Advance Praise

The Solar Food Dryer

Cheap. Simple. Easy to operate. The fuel is free. The product is tasty.
What's not to like? Read it.

— David Morris, Institute for Local Self-Reliance

Here is an important do-it-yourself book. Because so much petroleum is
used in the commercial growing and transport of food, we can expect that the
rising cost of petroleum will speed the rise of food prices. As a result, more and
more people will want to turn to solar drying of locally-grown foods in order to
reduce family food costs. I recommend this book as a valuable introduction to
this ancient but modern development in the preservation of food.

— Albert A. Bartlett, Professor Emeritus of Physics,
University of Colorado at Boulder

The Solar Food Dryer is a practical and handy guide — a step-by-step,
easy-to-follow manual to help US readers design, build and operate a solar food
dryer. In a time when people are increasingly concerned about the quality of
food they're eating, this book is an excellent guide, allowing readers to learn and
improve upon many age-old techniques to preserve and store summer's bounty.

— Tom Lawand, Solargetics Ltd.

THE
SOLAR
FOOD DRYER

Books for Wiser Living from

Mother Earth News

Today, more than ever beofre, our society is seeking ways to live more conscientiously. To help bring you the very best inspiration and information about greener, more sustainable lifestyles, New Society Publishers has joined forces with *Mother Earth News*. For more than 30 years, *Mother Earth News* has been North America's Original Guide to Living Wisely, creating books and magazines for people with a passion for self-reliance and a desire to live in harmony with nature. Across the countryside and in our cities, New Society Publishers and *Mother Earth News* are leading the way to a wiser, more sustainable world.

THE
SOLAR
FOOD DRYER

How to make and use your own
high-performance, sun-powered food dehydrator

Eben Fodor

NEW SOCIETY PUBLISHERS

Cataloging in Publication Data:
A catalog record for this publication is available from the National Library of Canada.

Cover design by Diane McIntosh. Photos: Eben Fodor.

Printed in Canada.
First printing December 2005.

Paperback ISBN-10: 0-86571-544-0
Paperback ISBN-13: 978-0-86571-544-8

Inquiries regarding requests to reprint all or part of *The Solar Food Dryer* should be addressed to New Society Publishers at the address below.

To order directly from the publishers, please call toll-free (North America) 1-800-567-6772, or order online at www.newsociety.com

Any other inquiries can be directed by mail to:
New Society Publishers
P.O. Box 189, Gabriola Island, BC V0R 1X0, Canada
1-800-567-6772

New Society Publishers' mission is to publish books that contribute in fundamental ways to building an ecologically sustainable and just society, and to do so with the least possible impact on the environment, in a manner that models this vision. We are committed to doing this not just through education, but through action. We are acting on our commitment to the world's remaining ancient forests by phasing out our paper supply from ancient forests worldwide. This book is one step toward ending global deforestation and climate change. It is printed on acid-free paper that is **100% old growth forest-free** (100% post-consumer recycled), processed chlorine free, and printed with vegetable-based, low-VOC inks. For further information, or to browse our full list of books and purchase securely, visit our website at: www.newsociety.com

NEW SOCIETY PUBLISHERS   www.newsociety.com

Contents

Acknowledgments xv
Introduction 1

Chapter 1: Food Drying Is More Fun in the Sun! 3
    Why Dry? 3
    Going Solar 4
    Is Solar Food Drying Right for Me? 6
    Why Haven't I Heard More about Solar Food Dryers? 6
    The Bigger Picture 7

Chapter 2: Harvesting Solar Energy 9
    The Power of the Sun: Capturing Solar Energy to Dry Food 9
    Solar Basics 10
    Geography and Seasons 11
    Climate and Weather Issues 17
    Atmospheric Clearness 17
    More Solar Facts 18

Chapter 3: Design Considerations for Solar Dryers 21
    Making Food Dry: Heat and Air Flow 21
    Direct Heating by the Sun 22

The Basic Solar Collector 24

The "Solar Fan" 26

Temperatures and Venting. 26

Collector Angle 26

Insulation and Double Glazing. 29

Reflectors 29

Weatherizing 29

Preventing Outdoor Pests 29

Backup Electric Heating 30

Maintenance and Cleaning 30

How Big a Dryer Do I Need? Size, Capacity and Portability 31

Materials. 31

Using Recycled Materials. 34

Types of Solar Dryers. 34

Chapter 4: Complete Instructions for Making Your Own Solar Dryer 47

SunWorks Solar Dryer Features 47

Assembly Instructions 50

Parts List for SunWorks Solar Food Dryer 51

Enhancements 74

Chapter 5: Putting Your Solar Dryer to Work 77

What to Dry 77

Food Preparation for Drying. 77

When to Dry 79

Backup Heating During Poor Weather 80

Operating Tips. 80

How Drying Preserves Food. 81

Drying Times and Temperatures 82

How Dry is Dry Enough? 82

Storing Dried Foods. 83

Nutrition and Food Quality 84

Pre-treating Foods to Prevent Darkening 86

Chapter 6: Favorite Dried Food Recipes 89

Appendix A: Sun Path Charts 97

Appendix B: Useful Solar Data 103

Appendix C: Handy Conversion Factors for Solar Energy 107

Appendix D: Glossary of Terms for Solar Energy 109

Appendix E: Resources for Solar Food Drying 113

Index 117

About the Author 121

Acknowledgments

Solar energy is both incredibly simple and surprisingly complex, so I am grateful for help from a couple of solar professionals. Thanks to Dr. Frank Vignola, Director of the Solar Energy Center at the University of Oregon, for preparing a set of custom sun path charts for this book and for generously sharing his knowledge of solar energy. Thanks to Daryl Myers, Senior Scientist at the National Renewable Energy Laboratory in Golden, Colorado, for help understanding and modeling the relationship between the sun and the amount of solar energy landing on various tilted surfaces. The result is a chart of solar energy gain on low tilt angles that has never been published before, as far as I know. Thanks to Dennis Scanlin for sharing his considerable experience with solar food dryers. Thanks are also due to the following folks for the information, ideas and references they shared with me: Dean Still, Jennifer Barker, Roger Ebbage, Kathy Ging, Chris Berner, Jeffry Heller and Gen MacManiman. Hand-drawn art is by graphic artist Jesse Springer of Eugene, Oregon.

Introduction

The summer bounty at this farmers market in Eugene, Oregon, is typical of a growing number of communities around the country.

This book is about the beauty and practicality of solar food drying — the elegant simplicity of allowing the sun to finish off its summer's work. In particular, it's about how to harness the sun's energy by building your own solar dryer that will deliver outstanding results.

Solar food drying is fun, easy and *free*. With renewable sunshine, you can dry as much as you like, as often as you like. Solar food drying is a far more practical way to dry your garden produce than most people would think. A good, high-performance solar dryer is designed to harness the sun efficiently and works amazingly well in almost any part of North America, and at most times of the year.

As an avid backyard organic gardener, I thoroughly enjoy being able to dry and preserve the extra bounty from my garden and small orchard with sustainable solar technology. Instead of trying to give away all those

1

extra tomatoes and zucchinis, they go into the dryer. I can also take full advantage of seasonal produce from the local farmers market by drying the things I don't grow (or don't grow enough of), such as strawberries, blueberries, peppers, and so forth. My solar food dryer has become an essential and delightful tool for capturing the summer's bounty and enjoying healthful produce throughout the year.

Chapters 1 through 3 are intended to give you a well-rounded understanding of solar food drying and the solar energy that powers it. These chapters are meant to enrich your solar food drying experience, not to overwhelm you. If you don't have patience for the details, feel free to skip ahead. If you already know a few things about solar food drying (or want to build now and read later), you can go right to Chapter 4 and follow the step-by-step guide to building your solar dryer!

Chapter 1: Food Drying is More Fun in the Sun addresses the practical questions about solar food drying: Why dry? Why use the sun? And will it really work for me?

Chapter 2: Harvesting Solar Energy will familiarize you with some of the basic principles of solar energy that will help you successfully capture the sun's energy to dry food. Generally, these are the same principles that apply to active and passive solar heating systems for space and water heating. This section includes some design guidelines and solar data that illustrate the power of the sun and the variation in solar energy by time-of-day, season, and latitude.

Chapter 3: Design Considerations for Solar Dryers introduces and describes the features that will make your solar dryer a big success. Some of the better dryer designs are described.

Chapter 4 provides complete, step-by-step instructions for building your own SunWorks solar food dryer from readily available new or recycled materials. A parts list, with lots of assembly photos and drawings, will guide you through the process.

Chapter 5: Putting Your Solar Dryer to Work tells how to get great results and maximize your enjoyment of your solar dryer. Operating tips, nutritional issues, and food storage methods are discussed.

Once you have begun solar food drying, a collection of favorite dried-food recipes in Chapter 6 will get you going right away.

The appendices provide additional solar energy and food drying resources and references that will help you become a solar food drying pro. If you run across a word in this book that you aren't familiar with, check the glossary in Appendix D.

CHAPTER 1

Food Drying is More Fun in the Sun!

Why Dry?

More and more people are discovering the joys and benefits of growing their own food and buying fresh, local produce. Garden foods are seasonal, resulting in the boom-and-bust cycle. First, you can't wait to savor your first vine-ripe tomato. In no time you've got more tomatoes than you can give away. Then frost hits and the party's over.

Some gardeners turn to canning and freezing to preserve their nutritious bounty. Drying is a third option that has some distinct advantages. Drying is simple and easy: If you can slice a tomato, you can dry food. Dried foods retain more nutrients than canned foods and don't require the energy of a freezer. Dried food is concentrated, reducing bulk and weight to ½ to $\frac{1}{15}$th that of hydrated food. Drying requires fewer containers and less storage space. A power failure (or mechanical failure) can

result in the loss of all your frozen foods, but your dried foods will be A-ok.

Dried foods are convenient and easy to handle. Use as much as you want, and put the rest back for later. Take them with you on hikes, camping, or vacations — they're light and hold up well under a wide range of conditions. Dried foods can last about as long as frozen foods, which are subject to freezer burn.

Drying can actually improve the flavor of many foods. Bananas are fantastic fruits, but dried bananas are heavenly. A Roma tomato is almost too bland to eat fresh, but dried it's a treat your tastebuds will savor. Watery Asian pears are sometimes a little disappointing. Dried, they are among the finest treats on the planet.

Indoor electric food dryers have become very popular in recent years. These dryers generally work well. But they do have some drawbacks. They require electricity around the clock — 100 to 600 Watts is typical. An electric dryer costs about one to two dollars per load for the electricity to operate it. These electricity costs eat into the savings of doing it yourself.

Electric dryers also take up vital counter space and release all the moisture, heat and odors indoors. The heat and moisture from electric dryers comes at the most unwelcome time of year — the summer harvest, when it's still hot outside. Sometimes the odors are pleasant, but when they continue for days and weeks, they become a nuisance and can attract pests, like ants and fruit flies, into your home. And there is the constant humming of the electric fan.

If you have a sunny area on your patio, deck, or back yard, a solar food dryer can produce outstanding results without any of these hassles.

Going Solar

Solar food dryers have zero operating costs. Dry all you want — it's free! Solar food dryers are easy to use and fairly easy to build — if you know just a few simple solar design concepts. Once you learn how to put the sun's energy to work, you can experiment with many possible designs. Or simply follow the detailed instructions provided here to build a high-performance solar dryer of your own.

Using the sun to dry food may be the oldest form of food preservation, dating back thousands of years. For many prehistoric people, dried fruits, berries, grains, fish, and meat were essential to surviving the cold winters. Hanging or laying food out in the open air and sunshine was the simplest method available for drying and preserving the food collected over the summer. The historic photo in Figure 1-1 shows the common Native American practice of using drying racks. Native Americans dried meat, fish, berries, and roots in the sun.

But simple outdoor sun drying leaves a lot of room for improvement. Your precious food will take a while to dry and will be subject to possible rotting and assault from rain, wind, dust, rodents, bugs, and, well, you get the idea. These problems are readily solved with a well-designed solar dryer that uses a few modern materials such as glass, plywood, screens, and adjustable vents.

While "solar dryer" could refer to a tray set out on your deck, in this book, the term is used to refer to a durable, enclosed, weatherproof design that takes advantage of basic solar energy design principles to efficiently and securely dry food. "Sun drying" refers to simply placing food out in the open sunshine to dry.

The solar food dryer stays outside and efficiently harnesses the sun's power to dry food much faster than ordinary sun drying. The sun has a surprising amount of energy and a solar food dryer is a great way to get acquainted with the impressive nature of solar power.

A well-designed solar dryer dries food quickly — typically in one to two days — by capturing the sun's energy to produce heat and move air across the food. Warmer air is lighter and rises (like a hot air balloon) in a process called natural convection. Natural convection can be used like a "solar fan" to speed drying.

This book features my own dryer design — the SunWorks SFD — which was originally constructed from scrap and recycled materials that I had on hand (and are widely available).

1-1: *Sun-Drying Fish at a Umatilla Indian Camp, on the Umatilla River in Oregon, 1903 by Lee Moorhouse (Courtesy of Special Collections and University Archives, University of Oregon Library System). This is a view of the camp of Billy Barnhart on the bluffs next to the Umatilla River. In the foreground two women stand at either end of a fish-drying rack made of wooden poles that is loaded with fish hung up to dry in the sun.*

This provided me with the added pleasure of minimizing consumption of natural resources. The design presented here is built with new materials to standardize the construction process. Once you have materials on hand, you can build this dryer in a weekend. Several other designs are illustrated to give you an idea of the range of design possibilities.

Designs for solar food dryers and solar cookers proliferated in the 1970s as interest in alternative energy and solar-heated homes peaked. Far too many of these designs used cardboard, tin foil and plastic wrap. The solar dryer designs described in this book are sturdy, dependable, highly effective, easy to use, weather resistant and will provide many years of enjoyment and savings.

Is Solar Food Drying Right for Me?

At this point, you may be wondering if you are heading down the right path. You may be asking "Is solar food drying really a good idea, and is it right for me?" Let me assure you that, with a little guidance from this book, you will never regret going solar. If you are not technically inclined and don't want to learn the details about solar energy, you will still be successful, because using solar energy is intuitive. You just have to do what's obvious. In fact it's hard to screw it up.

Occasionally I find disparaging comments about solar food drying, such as "solar dryers are not suitable for humid climates," or "solar dryers won't work in areas without lots of sunshine." A good solar dryer will work well in most of the world and anywhere in the Lower 48 states where you can get two days of sunshine in a row with some regularity. In fact, just about anywhere you can grow a successful outdoor vegetable garden, you can use a solar dryer.

Outdoor temperature and humidity levels have only minor impact on solar food drying. You can successfully dry foods in the muggiest climates and at outdoor temperatures down to about 45° F. Clouds, however, will diminish drying quite a bit. An overcast day will leave your solar dryer sputtering. For this reason, a backup electric heat option is a good idea to protect against unpredictable weather changes. (Electric backup is included in the plans for building the SunWorks dryer.)

Why Haven't I Heard More About Solar Food Dryers?

If solar food dryers are so great, why aren't lots of people using them? Solar food drying started to take off in the late 1970s when energy prices spiked and interest in solar technology peaked. There was quite a bit of experimentation, and many solar food dryer designs emerged. But with little research funding and no promotion, they never achieved much popular status. The 1980s and 1990s were periods of economic expansion and interest in energy conservation and renewable energies was all but forgotten.

But energy prices are heading skyward again, resulting in a broad reawakening the importance of sustainable alternative energies. Along with the growing awareness of our over-reliance on fossil fuels, we are seeing an increased interest in healthy eating, high-quality organic produce, local food production, and sustainable living. Solar food drying is an obvious part of the solutions to these challenges.

Another factor that may have held solar food drying back in the past was a perceived lack of convenience and performance. Designs for solar dryers have ranged from shoe boxes covered with plastic wrap (a good science experiment) to big bulky contraptions that have to be assembled every time they're used. There is a happy medium.

There is plenty of power in the sun to dry food quickly, so good performance simply requires proper design. Solar dryers can be highly effective and on par with the best electric dryers. Because solar dryers need to collect sunshine for power, they must have a certain bulkiness associated with the glazing area. The larger the capacity of the dryer, the more sunshine is needed to power it.

The SunWorks dryer described in this book was designed to be compact, lightweight, and portable, but still have enough capacity for the serious home gardener. Since there are many ways to harness the sun, a number of other good solar dryer designs are also described in this book. Everyone with a vegetable garden or a passion for locally grown produce should consider getting a solar food dryer. If you haven't been hearing about them yet, you soon will!

The Bigger Picture

I often get blank looks when I mention solar food drying to people. But then I ask them to think about how important food is, how dependent we are on importing foods from far away, how the quality of those foods is often not the best, and how our long-distance food supply depends on fossil fuels for shipping and storage. The alternative is to expand the local food supply. But when the local growing season is over, what can we do to extend our local self-reliance in a sustainable manner? It all starts to become clear: Solar food drying is the renewable energy solution to the local food supply challenge.

Sure, as long as fossil fuels remain cheap, lots of people will continue to buy winter grapes and plums from Chile, peppers from Mexico, tomatoes from artificially heated hothouses, and apples and pears from refrigerated storage warehouses. But this energy-intensive food supply system seems vulnerable and beyond our control. And the nutritional quality and safety of the food is often questionable. Solar food drying is simply the healthy, sustainable alternative. And it's ready to work for you today!

CHAPTER 2

Harvesting Solar Energy

The Power of the Sun:
Capturing Solar Energy to Dry Food

Each day the sun rises, warms the Earth back up, and powers the entire biosphere. There is plenty of extra sunshine available to dry your food. On a clear day, up to 1,000 Watts of solar energy are available for our use per square meter of area of the Earth's surface. This means that a solar food dryer with a horizontal window (or glazing) area of one square meter will have up to 1,000 Watts (3,413 Btu/hr) of solar power available to dry food. However, this is at noon on a clear summer day. Typical operating conditions for a solar dryer will vary depending on weather, geographic location, season, and of course, time of day.

Solar food drying is a great way to learn more about the sun and solar energy. By using a solar dryer you will gain an appreciation for the remarkable potential of this plentiful energy source. You will learn how to efficiently harness solar energy and put it to work preserving your food. And you will discover that it's easier than you might think.

Solar Weed Killer

If you happen to have an old, unused window around the house, you can use it as a solar weed killer. Simply place the window on a weedy area for one to two hours during mid-day in the summer. When you remove the window, the weeds will have turned brown and died — cooked by the sun. You can move the window around each day to kill another area of weeds. To get good results, the window must lie fairly flat and the frame must seal in the heat around the perimeter of the window by resting close to the ground (not for tall weeds).

Most of us have experienced the heat in our car after it has been sitting in the sun for a few hours. The car is acting as a primitive solar collector and can get quite hot. Imagine the potential for an efficient solar collector! To get more of a feeling for solar power, try the solar weed killer described in the sidebar.

Note: I have actually seen sources recommending that people dry food in their car by placing it on the dashboard. Yikes! This is a terrible idea. Not only will all the food moisture and odors end up in the car, but the car's odors and plasticizers will end up in your food.

Solar Basics

The rest of this chapter is devoted to giving you the solar energy basics that you will need to get the most out of your solar food drying experience. You will see how geography, seasons, and climate affect your solar drying potential.

Total available solar energy on a year-round basis peaks at the equator. The farther north or south you are from the equator, the less total solar energy is available over the year. Solar food drying is likely to be successful as far north as 50° north latitude. It may still be possible at higher latitudes (farther north), but with a

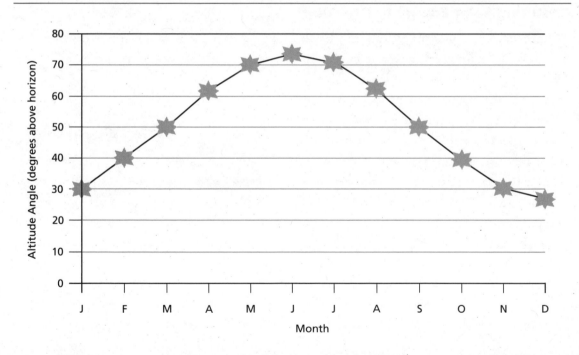

2-1: *Maximum sun angles at noon for the 21ˢᵗ day of each month at 40° north latitude*

more limited season, like June and July when solar radiation peaks.

On a clear day, the solar energy available at any given location is dependent on the angle of the sun relative to the horizon. A higher sun angle (solar altitude angle) results in more solar energy reaching your food dryer. For the northern hemisphere, the sun reaches its maximum solar altitude at solar noon on June 21st, the summer solstice. The solar altitude angle at noon is lowest on December 21st, the winter solstice. As you can see in Figure 2-1, there is quite a bit of variation in the peak sun angle over the year.

It's easy to see that there is a lot more sun to work with in the summer than winter.

Geography and Seasons

The sun travels across the sky each day in a path that varies throughout the year depending on the latitude of your location. Your latitude is the measure of how far you are from the Equator. The Equator is zero degrees (0°) latitude, with all latitude lines running parallel to the equator. The North Pole, for example, is 90° north latitude. The southern hemisphere is measured in *south* latitudes. Most of the contiguous United

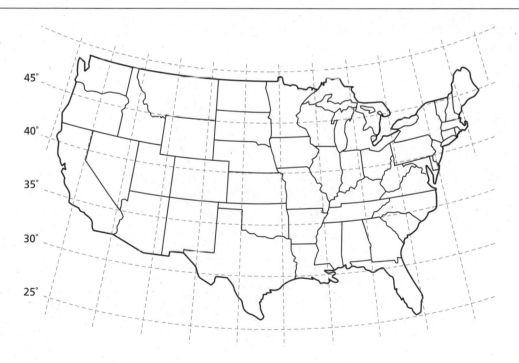

2-2: *Latitudes for contiguous American states*

States lie between about 30° and 49° north latitude. The 40° north latitude line is used here as a rough midpoint for the country, and some of the figures use 40° north latitude as a representative value. Use Figure 2-2 to find your approximate latitude, or consult a local map.

Movement of the Sun: Sun Path Charts

Once you know your latitude, you can determine the location of the sun in the sky at any time of day throughout the year with a sun path chart. They are very useful tools for designing or using any solar device. They are also useful in building design to locate windows and shading for day lighting and to take maximum advantage of passive solar space heating.

To help visualize a sun path chart, imagine yourself facing south and watching the sun travel across the sky, as in Figure 2-3. You would be seeing the sun begin its assent from low in the east, rise up towards a peak at 12 noon (when the sun is due south), and then descend into the western horizon. This journey would be one plot on a sun path chart. As shown in the illustration, the sun path is highest in summer and lowest in winter.

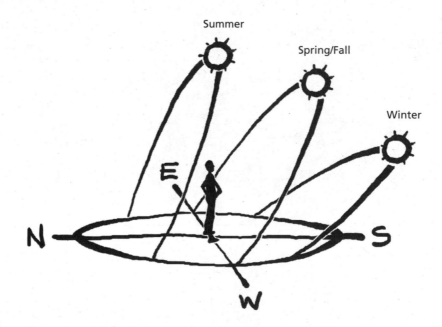

2-3: *Illustration of the sun's path for summer and winter*

As mentioned earlier, the relative height of the sun in the sky (or elevation) is represented by the altitude angle. *Altitude angle* measures the angle between the horizon and the location of the sun. If the sun is on the horizon, the altitude angle is 0°. If the sun is directly overhead, the altitude angle is 90°.

The sun's apparent movement from east to west can be measured with a compass or bearing angle to show how far east or west it is. To make this as simple as possible, due south has been set to be a bearing angle of 0°. Due east is -90° and due west is +90°. Now we can plot the course of the sun across the sky on a graph with altitude angle on the Y-axis and bearing angle on the X-axis, as shown in the example in Figure 2-4 for 40° north latitude.

The sun path chart plots the sun's course on a graph for the 21st day of each month to capture the movement of the sun throughout the year. The arc of the sun across the sky is highest during the summer solstice (June 21) and lowest during the winter solstice (December 21). Note that the sun's arc rises and falls

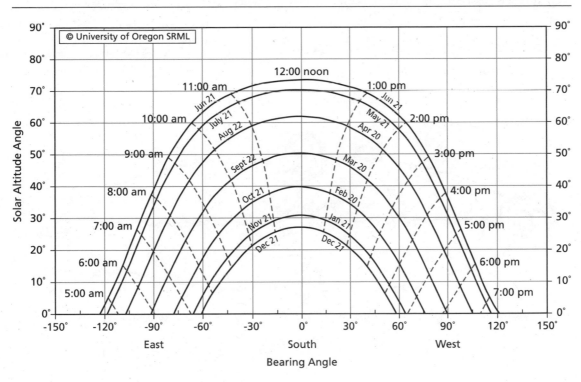

2-4: Sun path chart for 40° north latitude

symmetrically over the year so that both spring and fall equinoxes have the same sun path. Likewise the sun's path is the same for other dates that fall six months apart in the calendar like October 21 and February 20.

Sun paths are different for each latitude, so charts are provided in Appendix A for every 5° of latitude from 30° north to 50° north, covering most of the Lower 48 states and southern Canada. The sun's path is the same for all locations along the same latitude.

The sun path charts provided here go one step further than simply plotting paths. The hours of the day are also plotted so that you can determine where the sun will be at any time of day. These hours are given in solar time, which is similar to clock time, but varies by about ±15 minutes throughout the year. Twelve noon solar time is when the sun is highest in the sky (high noon). Solar time does not change with daylight savings time, so you would need to add an hour to solar time when savings time is in effect.

Seasonal Variations in Solar Energy

The Earth's axis of rotation is tilted 23.5° relative to the sun. As the Earth orbits the sun, this tilt causes the seasons to change. As shown in Figure 2-5, the northern hemisphere gets the most sun on the summer solstice, June 21,

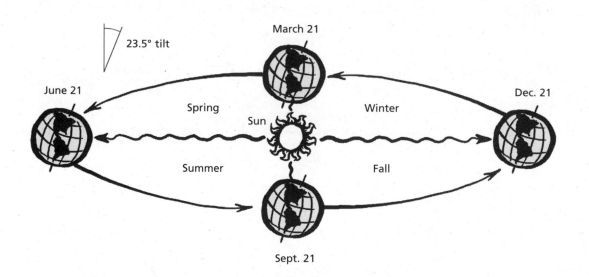

2-5: *Seasons result from Earth's tilted rotation around the sun*

marking the beginning of summer. The winter solstice and the two equinoxes (fall and spring) indicate the beginning of the three other seasons. Remember the Tropic of Cancer and the Tropic of Capricorn? They are located at 23.5° north and south latitude from the equator, respectively, and mark the farthest extent at which the sun passes directly overhead. All areas outside of the tropics will have peak sun angles that are less than 90° throughout the year.

The actual solar energy reaching the surface of the Earth on a clear day varies considerably over the year, as shown in Figure 2-6. Note that clear-sky data are used here because this is the most appropriate for solar food drying. It's a selective activity that will generally be performed during good weather, and not when it's overcast or raining.

The total solar energy reaching the Earth's surface is a combination of *direct radiation* and *diffuse sky radiation*. Direct radiation comes directly from the sun and is the kind we think of when we refer to "sunshine." About 10 percent of the total radiant energy is diffuse radiation — solar radiation that has been reflected off dust

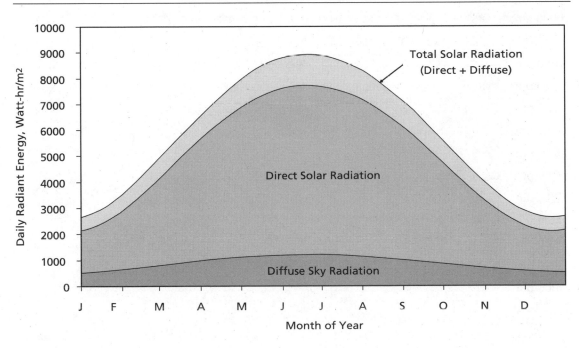

2-6: *Variation in solar energy on a horizontal surface with clear skies over the year at 40° north latitude*

	Dec	Jan	Feb	Mar	Apr	May	Jun	Jul	Aug	Sep	Oct	Nov	Dec
12:00 am	0	0	0	0	0	0	0	0	0	0	0	0	0
1:00 am	0	0	0	0	0	0	0	0	0	0	0	0	0
2:00 am	0	0	0	0	0	0	0	0	0	0	0	0	0
3:00 am	0	0	0	0	0	0	0	0	0	0	0	0	0
4:00 am	0	0	0	0	0	0	0	0	0	0	0	0	0
5:00 am	0	0	0	0	0	77	129	111	31	0	0	0	0
6:00 am	0	0	0	42	179	280	326	309	230	106	0	0	0
7:00 am	0	15	114	250	389	481	520	505	435	316	174	46	0
8:00 am	152	182	305	446	581	664	696	682	620	508	366	225	152
9:00 am	301	334	464	608	740	814	840	828	773	667	525	378	301
10:00 am	407	442	577	724	852	921	943	931	882	780	638	488	407
11:00 am	463	498	636	784	911	976	996	985	938	839	697	545	463
12:00 pm	463	498	636	784	911	976	996	985	938	839	697	545	463
1:00 pm	407	442	577	724	852	921	943	931	882	780	638	488	407
2:00 pm	301	334	464	608	740	814	840	828	773	667	525	378	301
3:00 pm	152	182	305	446	581	664	696	682	620	508	366	225	152
4:00 pm	0	15	114	250	389	481	520	505	435	316	174	46	0
5:00 pm	0	0	0	42	179	280	326	309	230	106	0	0	0
6:00 pm	0	0	0	0	0	77	129	111	31	0	0	0	0
7:00 pm	0	0	0	0	0	0	0	0	0	0	0	0	0
8:00 pm	0	0	0	0	0	0	0	0	0	0	0	0	0
9:00 pm	0	0	0	0	0	0	0	0	0	0	0	0	0
10:00 pm	0	0	0	0	0	0	0	0	0	0	0	0	0
11:00 pm	0	0	0	0	0	0	0	0	0	0	0	0	0

2-7: *Radiation square showing approximate hourly average radiation (in watts/m²) on a horizontal surface for clear skies at 40° north latitude (solar time)*

and moisture in the sky. Diffuse radiation comes from the entire sky.

Another interesting way to look at the potential solar energy over the year is the *radiation square*. Figure 2-7 shows a radiation square for 40° north latitude. For each month of the year, the radiation square shows the average radiant energy available for every hour of the day. In this way it is possible to see approximately how much solar energy you have to work with at any time of the year.

Climate and Weather Issues

Successful solar food drying requires one to two days of sunshine with daytime temperatures of around 50° F (10° C) or above. These conditions exist everywhere in the continental US and in most places where people live. The Pacific Northwest is one of the rainiest areas of the US, but has enough sunny days during summer and early fall to be perfectly suitable. However, climates that are perpetually overcast are not suitable. If you live in a place like Nova Scotia or Scotland, solar food drying is probably not for you. On the other hand, if you live in the Southwest, you may be able to dry food with the sun all year long.

Weather is often unpredictable. Clouds can move in and put an end to your solar party. Clouds and haze will significantly reduce your solar power supply. To prevent your drying operation from stalling completely, a backup heat source is a good idea. A backup electric heating system is useful in all but the most sunny and arid climates. (Backup heating is addressed further in Chapter 3.)

Figure 2-8 shows the actual average daily solar energy falling on a horizontal surface during the month of June for 239 monitoring locations in the United States. Additional maps are provided in Appendix B for different times of year. This map will give you an idea of the overall solar potential for your location relative to other parts of the country. Keep in mind that these averaged figures reflect the local climate and include cloudy, rainy, and hazy days as well as clear, sunny days. Since you will presumably be doing your solar food drying on sunny days, these figures do not show the full potential solar energy on these days. (Note: To convert to metric units [watt-hours/ m^2/day], multiply Btu/ft^2/day by 3.15. Other useful conversions can be found in Appendix C.)

Atmospheric Clearness

Atmospheric clearness is affected by the amount of dust and moisture in the air, and varies geographically and seasonally. It is generally within about ten percent of the average clearness for most of the US. This means that the amount of solar energy passing through the atmosphere can be ten percent higher or lower than average, depending on clearness. For example, the Southeast (Florida and the Gulf Coast) has low clearness in the winter, while the Southwest (Colorado, Utah, Arizona and New Mexico) has high clearness in the summer. The normal range of clearness in the US does not vary enough to significantly affect the success of solar drying.

More Solar Facts

Solar radiation spans the spectrum from short-wavelength ultraviolet to visible light to long-wavelength infrared. Visible light is approximately 47 percent of the incident extraterrestrial solar radiation. Visible wavelengths are from 380 to 780 nanometers. The infrared portion of the spectrum, with wavelengths greater than 780 nanometers, accounts for another 46 percent of the incident energy. The ultraviolet portion of the spectrum is comprised of wavelengths below 380 nanometers and accounts for 7 percent of the extraterrestrial solar radiation.

The "solar constant" is the amount of solar energy reaching the Earth's atmosphere, about 1,367 W/m² (±3 percent). Approximately 75

2-8: *Actual average total daily solar energy in June on a horizontal surface (Btu/ft²/day).*
Source: National Renewable Energy Laboratory

percent of the sun's radiation passes through the Earth's atmosphere and reaches the surface. The rest is either absorbed or reflected by the moisture and dust in the atmosphere. The amount reaching the surface is about 1000 Watts/m². The sun is neither a solid nor a gas, but plasma. This plasma is gaseous near the surface, but denser towards the sun's fusion core. At the surface the effective temperature is 5,800° Kelvin (10,000° F or 5,500° C).

All of the energy that we detect as light and heat originates in nuclear fusion reactions deep inside the sun's high temperature core. This core extends about one quarter of the way from the center of the sun to its surface where the temperature is around 15 million degrees Kelvin (or 27 million degrees Fahrenheit).*

The southern hemisphere is a mirror image of the northern hemisphere in terms of solar energy and sun angles. The highest sun angle and longest day of the year in the north will occur on June 21. In the southern hemisphere this day will have the lowest sun angle and is the shortest day of the year. Likewise, December 21 will be the longest summer day in the southern hemisphere, but the shortest in the north. Total solar radiation at 40° north latitude on a clear summer day will be similar to a summer day at 40° south latitude. At the equinox, both north and south latitudes will receive similar solar radiation.

COURTESY NASA

2-9: *Sun's distance from Earth: 93 million miles (150 million km) on average*

*Celsius = Kelvin - 273°

CHAPTER 3

Design Considerations for Solar Dryers

To get the most enjoyment and best results from your solar food dryer, it must perform on a number of levels. Of course it must get your food dry in a reasonable time, but it must also be functional, reliable, easy to use, sanitary, weatherproof, pest proof, and usually portable.

This chapter covers the basic design features of a successful solar food dryer. Whether you are building the SunWorks SFD shown in this book or designing your own, you will want to review the key design qualities covered here.

Making Food Dry: Heat and Air Flow

Generally the trick to quality food drying is to do it as quickly as possible without overheating the food. This requires the right amount of two things: heat and air movement.

Heat (and Temperature)

Heat does two critical things to speed up drying. First, it raises the temperature of the air, enabling it to hold more moisture. Second, it warms the food, increasing the "vapor pressure" of the liquid water in the food. This means that increasing the temperature of the food increases the rate at which water evaporates into the surrounding air. The more heat and the higher the temperature, the faster drying can occur. Too much heat, though, and your food will get cooked or even burned. Solar dryers rarely get hot enough to burn food, but they can easily get to 160° F (71° C) or more, effectively pasteurizing and cooking the food.

A good solar dryer can heat the air 50° to 80° F (10° to 26° C) above the outdoor (ambient) temperature. This is referred to as the "ΔT" (delta-T), or temperature difference between ambient air and heated air. It means that if it's

85° F (29.5° C) outside, the dryer can get to 135° to 165° F (57° to 74° C) inside. The ΔT is one performance measure of a solar dryer. With plenty of sun, some dryers can reach a ΔT of 100° F (38° C) or more. Dryer temperatures can be controlled with adjustable vents, so the higher temperatures are achieved with the vents partially closed.

Air Flow

Air movement is the second essential element of drying. It carries the moist, saturated air away from the food and replaces it with dry, heated air that can absorb more water. If you had an unlimited heat source, then the more air movement, the faster things would dry. But given a fixed heat input from the sun, air flow should be kept at a level that will allow the air to be heated at least 30° F (17° C). This assures that the air will rapidly absorb moisture from the food. If there is too much air flow, the air is not warmed enough. With too little air flow, the air becomes too moist (saturated) and doesn't absorb more moisture from the food.

Direct Heating by the Sun

An object sitting in the sun will be much warmer than a similar object sitting in the shade, even though the outdoor air temperature is the same in both locations. This is fairly obvious to anyone who spends time outdoors — it just feels warmer in the sun (and cooler in the shade). The effective temperature in direct sunlight is referred to as the *sol-air temperature*. The sol-air temperature is about 20° F (11° C) higher than ambient air temperature. The effective *sol-air* temperature can range from 10° to 30° F above shade temperatures depending on factors such as the color or darkness of the object and the cooling effect of wind or air flow. (Weather temperatures are always measured in the shade for consistency.)

You can take advantage of this effect to dry food faster, just like countless other cultures have in the past. Food placed in direct sunlight (even under a glass cover) will get about 20° F (11° C) warmer than food that is shaded. The effective increase in temperature speeds up drying

---

Humid climate? No problem.

Consider a typical muggy summer day where the outdoor temperature is 85° F (29° C) with 80 percent relative humidity. Food would dry very slowly if left in the open outdoors because the humid air is already close to being saturated with moisture. At 80% humidity, this air can absorb only a small amount of additional moisture before becoming saturated (100% relative humidity).

By heating this same outdoor air to 120° F (49° C), the relative humidity of the air is reduced to 28 percent. The capacity of this heated air for holding moisture is more than three times greater than it was at 85°. This is why solar dryers work fine in humid climates (just like electric dryers do).

considerably. To help understand this, think about drying laundry outside on a clothesline. If half the laundry is in the sun and the other half in the shade, the laundry in the sun will dry much faster, even though the air temperature is the same for both. A solar dryer that allows most, or all, of the food to get direct solar heating will dry food significantly faster than one that doesn't (assuming that both dryers are identical in every other respect). Generally, I find that faster drying yields better quality food, in terms of both flavor and appearance.

Many solar dryer designs do take advantage of this principle. However, some designs keep the food in the shade based on the belief that sunlight may reduce nutrients. These are

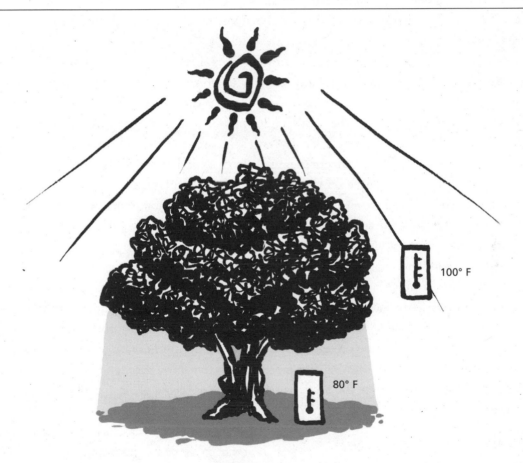

3-1: *The effective temperature with direct sunlight is about 20° F (11° C) higher than in the shade*

referred to as *indirect* solar dryers in this book, because the sun must heat the air first and then the air heats the food. A thorough search of all the nutritional and agricultural research journals dating back more than 30 years, however, found no studies pertaining to this effect, and no articles citing such studies. One contemporary study made an incidental finding that there was no effect from ambient light on the nutrients in dried food stored for 13 months when compared with food kept in the dark (see *Storing Dried Foods* in Chapter 5). The effect of sunlight on nutrients is probably minor and may be insignificant for the short one- to two-day drying period. Furthermore, the glass and other glazing materials used with solar dryers block most of the ultraviolet light from the sun, reducing any effect it may have on the nutritional content of the food.

If you are concerned about nutrients in your food, focus on the quality and freshness of the food, food handling and storage (before drying), minimal processing (by avoiding cooking, blanching or overheating foods), keeping drying times fairly short, storing dried foods properly, and final food preparations before eating, such as rehydrating, cooking and reheating. For more information on this topic, see the sections on nutrition and food storage in Chapter 5.

The Basic Solar Collector

The basic solar collector captures the sun's radiant energy and converts it to useful heat. It starts with an enclosure, or box, that surrounds the air or material to be heated. Solar energy is collected via a window (or glazing) that allows the radiant energy to enter the collector, but doesn't allow the heated air to leave. Once the radiant energy enters the collector, it strikes one of the dark surfaces inside and is absorbed and converted to heat. Some radiant energy will also be reflected. A good collector absorbs most of the solar energy and minimizes reflection.

A flat (not glossy) black surface will absorb and convert about 96 percent of the solar energy directly to heat. The remaining four percent will be reflected to other surfaces and some will be reflected out of the collector and lost. A black metal sheet is the most common surface for solar energy absorption because the metal will distribute and transfer the heat evenly throughout the collector. This is referred to as the "absorber plate."

Most people are likely to be familiar with the solar collectors used for domestic hot water heating. These systems run water through tubes embedded in the absorber plate. Typically an electric pump is used to circulate the water. As the water flows through the tubes, it is heated by the absorber plate, and the heated water is then stored in a water tank. Cooler water from the bottom of the tank is circulated back to the solar collector by the pump and heated. (The need for freeze protection complicates this process and usually means that water circulated through the solar collector contains an antifreeze and therefore must be separated from potable water by a heat exchanger.)

Solar collectors can be tilted towards the south to increase the amount of solar energy collected. The degree of the tilt angle can be optimized for the location and conditions under which the collector will be used. The solar collectors that most people are familiar with are used for hot water and space heating and are positioned to maximize solar input over the entire year. This is *not* the correct tilt angle for solar food dryers, however, as you will see.

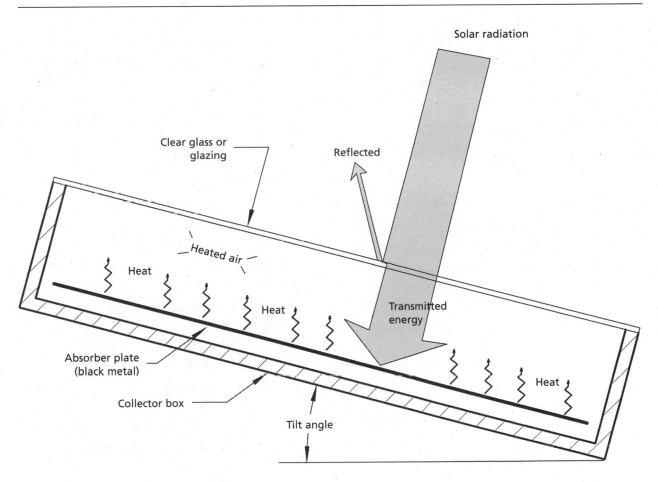

3-2: *Basic solar collector*

The "Solar Fan"

Once we have an efficient solar collector that generates lots of heat, the next step is to put the heat to work. For food drying, we want to heat the outside air entering the dryer to a sufficient temperature (100° to 150° F [38° to 65° C]) and move it across our food to remove moisture. This is where the design of a solar food dryer sinks or swims. Enough air must move through the dryer to carry out moisture. Too much air flow lowers the temperature of the dryer, slowing the drying process. Too little airflow and the moisture is trapped in the dryer and may end up condensing inside.

To move air, we can use a "solar fan." The sun's energy drives the wind. Its heating of the atmosphere produces gentle breezes, as well as driving storms. This same dynamic can be put to work in your dryer. The solar fan employs the simple concept that warm air rises. When air is warmed, it expands and becomes lighter than surrounding air. Like a hot-air balloon, it wants to go up. If we create an airflow path that allows cool outside air to enter at the bottom of our dryer and warm air to exit at the top, we have created the necessary conditions for the solar fan to work. This principle is referred to as "natural convection," but it may also be called "thermosiphoning," "updraft" or "the chimney effect." As the sun heats the air inside the dryer, it will rise and exit the vent at the top. This draws in cool air at the bottom to replace the air that is leaving. The hotter the

dryer gets, the faster the air will flow. Voila! A solar fan with no electricity needed. Ideally we want the solar fan to "blow" heated air across our food for faster drying. This means that the air flow path should cross as much of the food as possible.

Temperatures and Venting

To make it possible to adjust the temperature inside the dryer, we need an adjustable venting system. The best place for this is at the top of the dryer, to control the exit of warm air. Since the warm air inside the dryer is buoyant and wants to rise, it won't leave the dryer through a bottom vent. So bottom vents can be left open. There are lots of possible arrangements to vary venting with sliding or hinged vent doors.

If the adjustable vents on a solar dryer are closed and the unit is left in midday sun, it can get quite hot. If there is food in it, it can get cooked or even slightly burned. This problem can be avoided by creating small vent holes at the top that allow just enough air flow to keep things from overheating.

Collector Angle

In the northern hemisphere, solar collectors are tilted towards the south (and tilted north, in the southern hemisphere) to increase the amount of solar energy captured. The amount of tilt is based on a number of factors, including the time of year at which the collector will be operating. For example, a solar collector intended for winter space heating would have a steep angle to capture more of the low winter sun. A solar food dryer, however, operates primarily in the summer, and therefore requires a lower angle.

Solar water heating systems and solar photovoltaic (electric generation) systems must operate year-round and will have their tilt angle set at a compromise between optimal summer and winter angles. The optimal angle for full-time solar collectors varies depending on the latitude for each location. The ideal angle for maximum solar gain over the entire year can be estimated by taking the latitude of the location and subtracting 15 degrees. A collector located at 45 degrees latitude (Minneapolis) would therefore have a tilt of 30 degrees (45 - 15 = 30). A collector at 30 degrees latitude (New Orleans) would have a collector angle of 15 degrees.

Tilt is important for expensive solar water heating systems and photovoltaic systems that must capture as much solar energy as possible over a 20-year service life in order to be cost effective. However, tilt angle is much less important for a solar food dryer, and there is much more flexibility in choosing the tilt angle. In fact, any angle from horizontal (0°) to vertical (90°) can be made to work for a food dryer. Solar food dryers are most likely to be used in summer when the fresh produce is available and the sun is high in the sky. They will generally not be operated in winter, when sun angles are lowest. So they don't need to be angled in the same way as other solar systems that must operate all year.

Figure 3-3 shows the amount of daily solar radiation collected at various tilt angles throughout the year for 40° north latitude. You can use this graph to see which tilt angle will give you the most solar energy at the time of year when you will be doing most of your drying. The main food drying season is shown on the graph as running from May through October to cover harvest times for a fairly wide range of crops. If you are planning on drying only foods that are grown locally, this will be your food drying window of opportunity.

The graph in Figure 3-3 shows why traditional solar collector tilt angles are not appropriate for most food drying. The collected solar energy during the peak sunshine of early summer (around June 21) is greatest for a horizontal surface (tilt angle of 0°). A horizontal surface will actually collect more solar energy than a 30° tilt for more than three months of the year. A tilt angle of 10°, 15°, or 20° will outperform the 30° tilt for about four months of the year, most of which is during the main food drying season.

There are no rigid design guidelines for tilt angles for solar food dryers. The bottom line is whether or not they dry food quickly. The range of suitable tilt angles for a solar food dryer is limited mostly by practical considerations. A horizontal collector will not drain rain water, which could allow food to get wet. A collector with an angle steeper than 30° will be wasting sunshine during the prime summer operating time.

The practical range of angles for tilting a food dryer is from about 10° to 30°. Within this range, lower tilt angles will collect more energy in the summer and higher angles will collect more energy in the fall. The tilt angle for the SunWorks SFD is 12°. This angle was selected primarily because it allows for optimal air flow within the dryer.

If you are planning to do most of your drying in late August (when the tomato harvest peaks, for example), tilt angles from 0° to 45° all perform about the same. If you plan to dry earlier crops like strawberries, peas, carrots, or beans, your harvest may peak in June or July, and you will get more solar energy from a lower tilt angle (from 0° to 20°). Late season harvests of apples,

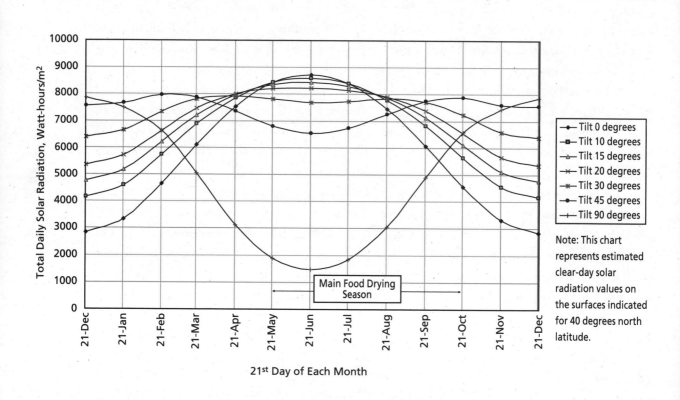

Note: This chart represents estimated clear-day solar radiation values on the surfaces indicated for 40 degrees north latitude.

3-3: *Comparison of solar energy on various south-facing tilted surfaces for 40° north latitude*

pears and grapes may peak in September and October, and your dryer will get the most solar power from higher tilt angles of 20° to 30°. If you plan on drying all types of crops throughout the harvest season, you may want a mid-range tilt of 10° to 20° for optimal solar gain.

Since this graph was compiled for 40° north latitude, you may want to make some adjustment for your location. If you are far north of this latitude, you will generally benefit from more tilt angle. While if you are far south of 40°, you will benefit from less tilt. Keep in mind that the overall functionality of your dryer design will be more important than having an ideal tilt angle.

Insulation and Double Glazing

High-performance solar collectors, like those used for domestic water heating systems, use double glazing (two-layered glass panes) and an insulated collector box to keep as much heat in the collector as possible. This is important for water heaters that must be able to heat water in the middle of winter. However, food dryers don't operate under the same demanding conditions. Most of the solar energy goes directly to heating the air flowing through the food dryer, and only a small fraction of the heat leaks out of the glazing or through the cabinet. The modest performance gains from adding double glazing and insulation generally do not justify the added cost of materials and extra weight. However, there is still plenty of room for experimentation in this area.

Reflectors

Reflectors can be used to boost the solar energy entering your dryer. The idea is simply to bounce more solar radiation into the collector with a mirror or foil-covered reflective surface. A reflector can be mounted on the top, sides or bottom of the collector and adjusted to direct its light into the glazing area. Reflectors are often used with solar cookers to help achieve the high temperatures (300° to 400° F [148° to 204° C]) needed for cooking. Reflectors have not been widely used with food dryers, but they may be useful to extend the drying season into late fall and winter.

Weatherizing

Solar foods dryers live outside, so they must be able to endure the elements without falling apart or harming your food. This means that rain should drain off without entering the dryer and getting the food wet. This is just a practical consideration and does not necessitate airtight or watertight construction methods. Materials should be selected that can hold up under rain and sun for many years. Plywood used for the cabinet should have exterior-grade glues. The legs of the dryer should be made from cedar or a treated wood that can survive ground contact without rotting.

Preventing Outdoor Pests

The food in your dryer may be of interest to a wide variety of animals and bugs, but proper design and a few tricks will keep them away. All vent openings must be screened to keep out flies and yellow jackets. Sturdy construction and latches on the loading door will keep your food safe from raccoons. If ants or cockroaches are a problem, having the dryer up on legs (rather than a tabletop design), makes the solution easy. Place each leg in a paper cup, bowl or plastic carton and add an inch or two of water. You have effectively put a moat around your dryer. The legs will soak up the water eventually, so check it occasionally.

Another approach is to dust the legs with diatomaceous earth. This is a natural powder made from sea-floor deposits of tiny crustaceans (diatoms). It's harmless to humans and pets but disables and kills ants and some other pests by dehydrating them. Diatomaceous earth only works when dry — once it gets wet, you will need to re-apply.

Backup Electric Heating

A backup electric heating system is not required for successful solar food drying, but it is a great option. The main drawback to solar food drying is the unpredictability of sunshine. If you plan to dry lots of your precious, high-quality garden produce, you want dependable results. After planting, cultivating, and harvesting the food and then washing, cutting, and loading the dryer, you will not be happy to see your hard work rotting in a solar dryer because the weather turned. This sort of hassle and waste will quickly detract from the joys of solar drying.

A backup electric heating option solves this problem and significantly improves the usefulness of your dryer. Not only can you dry dependably during the main food drying season, you can also dry during marginal times of year (using both limited sun and electric heat), or in the middle of winter (on electricity only). This flexibility and dependability adds a major dimension to solar drying, and you will still be saving lots of energy and money by using solar energy whenever it's available. If you live in the sunny Southwest or in the tropics, backup heating may not be as useful. Otherwise, it's highly recommended.

A simple heating element can be made from standard incandescent electric light bulbs. These lights are only 5 percent efficient as light sources. The other 95 percent is turned into heat. This makes them efficient heaters! If the light is also converted to heat within the dryer, then they are 100 percent efficient heaters. Heat output can be adjusted by selecting a bulb wattage that is appropriate. A 100-watt bulb will generate 5 watts of light energy and 95 watts of heat.

Maintenance and Cleaning

I keep my food dryer as clean as possible, but let's face it, food drying can be messy at times. Juicy fruit and tomatoes may drip onto the bottom. Concentrated fruit sugars from grapes may drip like honey. So, you will need to be able to access and clean your dryer at some point. It may only be necessary once a year, but a good dryer design is easy to hose out or scrub inside when needed.

The outside of the glass or glazing material, on the other hand, will need to be cleaned regularly. Dirt, dust and pollen will block precious solar rays from getting into your dryer. I clean my dryer glazing at least every couple of loads. The underside of the glazing needs to be cleaned once or twice a year, because dust and condensate will accumulate there.

How Big a Dryer Do I Need? Portability, Capacity and Size

A major consideration in the design of a solar food dryer is the *convenience factor*. If your dryer is not easy to use, you may find that you're simply not using it very much. There are probably a few old, homemade solar dryers sitting in storage that aren't getting used because they are just too big and heavy to move, or too much trouble to set up.

The best design will be ready to go when you are. It should be fairly light, easy to transport and have little or no setup time. And it should be compact and easy to store, either outside or in a garage or garden shed. I leave mine outside and just put a tarp over it when I know I won't be using it for a while.

It may sound appealing to build a dryer with a huge capacity. But a bigger capacity equals bulkier size, more weight, and extra cost. Don't overbuild your dryer or you risk ending up with an unused piece of "yard art."

Consider how much food you are likely to have on hand at one time and how much time you want to spend preparing and loading the food. The 6-pound capacity of the SunWorks SFD is plenty for most home users. Processing and loading 6 pounds of tomatoes or apples takes about 30 to 45 minutes. Twelve pounds would take twice as long.

Since you can dry a new load of food every two days, consider how much food your garden will produce in two days as a measure of how much capacity you might need. If you find that you don't have enough capacity in your dryer, having a second dryer may be the best way to go.

Materials

To produce a quality food dryer, you'll want to select materials that will hold up well in the outdoor environment. Any wood that contacts the ground (like the dryer legs) should be rot-resistant, like cedar. Treated wood should not be used in any area that has contact with food, or that may come in contact with your hands during loading and unloading of the dryer. Untreated pine, hemlock or fir wood will last for many years outdoors, as long as it's not in contact with the ground. Exterior-grade plywood is an excellent material for making a sturdy, lightweight cabinet.

The two materials of particular interest in the solar food dryer are the glazing and the food screens.

Glazing

Any clear or translucent material that transmits a high percentage of solar radiation is a candidate for solar food dryer glazing. Listed below are some of the possibilities.

Glass is one of the best solar glazing materials. A single pane of clear window glass transmits 86 to 92 percent of incident solar radiation, and filters out most of the higher frequency UV radiation. One of the best features of glass is that it's easy to clean and does not tend to get scratched. It holds up well outdoors, does not yellow or become hazy and can last indefinitely, if not broken. It's also readily available at most hardware stores and is about the lowest-cost material that can be used for a durable application like a dryer. On the down side, glass is brittle and can break fairly easily. It's also heavy and has sharp edges. Tempered glass breaks without the sharp edges, but it costs more than regular untempered glass and isn't significantly stronger.

Fiberglass-reinforced polyester is a thin, durable sheet that is lightweight and reasonably priced. This material has been widely used for solar collector applications. It transmits 84 to 90 percent of solar radiation. It's translucent, so it won't provide a good view of your food, if that is part of your plan. It's very resistant to breakage. It is flexible with little structural strength so it may sag in the middle if not stretched tightly or supported, and will also expand when heated. (See *Resources* in Appendix E for sources.)

Polycarbonate sheet is transparent and may be the closest alternative to glass. This is the same material that most sunglasses and safety glasses are made from. It's hard and tough, and won't scratch easily. It's a rigid material that doesn't bend easily, and it's lighter than glass. Polycarbonate is available in clear sheets for outdoor applications like greenhouses. It comes with a UV-resistant coating on one side that blocks most UV and protects the material from aging. It has a high thermal expansion (like many plastics), which can make mounting and sealing difficult. Proper mounting should allow for movement due to thermal expansion. This material is available at some hardware stores and is fairly expensive.

Acrylic (Plexiglass) is available in clear sheets. It's not nearly as strong or hard as polycarbonate, yet costs almost as much. It will scratch easily and yellows with time, reducing its performance for solar applications. It has similar thermal expansion characteristics to polycarbonate.

Plastic films are generally not sturdy or durable enough for solar dryer applications; however, some designs still call for them. They can provide a cheap and quick glazing material for experimenting with solar energy, or act as a temporary glazing until you can find something better. The best plastic film is probably **polyester** (Mylar). It's clear, very tough, fairly heat tolerant and doesn't stretch or sag. Some polyester films are designed especially for outdoor applications, so these would be the ones to consider. The most common plastic film is **polyethylene.** It is sometimes used for cold frames or as a covering for temporary greenhouses. While cheap, polyethylene is not very durable and will fall apart within a couple of years.

Food Screens

The screens that the food rests on in the dryer must be made from a mesh that allows plenty of airflow. The screens should be made from an inert (non-reactive), food-safe material that can withstand dryer temperatures as high as 200° F (93° C). Good screens should not stick to food and will be easy to clean. Furthermore, the material should not stretch or sag when heated and loaded with food. All together, this is a pretty tall order, and few materials can make the grade.

Certain popular screen materials are not suitable for food applications because they are reactive. Galvanized metal screen and wire mesh, for example, contain zinc and other metals that could oxidize and dissolve into the food. Aluminum screens may be suitable for many foods, but can react with the acids in tomatoes.

Polypropylene screens are available in food-safe materials and are strong and easy to clean. They come in various forms, ranging from a fine screen material that can be used as the main screen on drying racks, or as thicker, coarser screen inserts that can be placed on top of other drying racks.

Fiberglass window screens work well in food dryer applications but may not be safe for food contact. Fiberglass screens are made from woven fiberglass coated with vinyl. While vinyl is safely used in many food-contact applications, the plasticizers used with window screens are not FDA approved for food uses. If you are using fiberglass screen in your dryer, consider placing the food on polypropylene tray inserts.

Stainless steel screens are expensive and hard to work with in terms of cutting and bending. Stainless steel comes in many grades, depending on the alloys it is made with, so it's important to use a food-grade stainless. Some grades may leach metals and flavors into foods. More and more of the stainless screen material is made in China, so it's difficult to be certain of alloy content. Another issue with stainless is that it is reflective, so it will bounce some solar energy back out of the dryer, if your design uses direct solar heating.

Screen options are rather limited right now, but with growing interest in solar food drying we can hope for more products to emerge in the near future. Other materials may be suitable for solar dryer screens, including nylon, polyester, Teflon-coated fiberglass and natural fibers.

Using Recycled Materials

Using recycled or reclaimed materials for constructing your solar dryer is a great way to reduce consumption of natural resources and save money at the same time. Window glazing and screens are likely to be the most expensive part of a solar dryer, but it's possible to find them for next to nothing at recycling centers. If there is no recycling center nearby, try calling a window replacement or home weatherizing company. Windows and screens from old aluminum storm windows and storm doors are best, but wood frames will work too. Always replace the old screen material with new material — preferably polypropylene screening — before using it in your dryer (see Chapter 4 for screen installation instructions). Plywood scraps, which are useful in making the cabinet, are plentiful at construction sites where exterior-grade sheathing is cut out for windows and doors. Avoid particle board, though, which is not as strong or durable. You may be able to find cedar boards left over from decking and fencing projects. Avoid using treated wood in any part of the dryer that may contact food. More information on using recycled materials is provided with the instructions in Chapter 4.

Types of Solar Dryers

There is a wide range of solar dryer designs, and probably just about all of them work to some extent. Each design may have certain advantages. So the question is not so much "Will this work?" as "How well will this work?" and "Is this the best dryer for my needs?" What distinguishes the various dryer designs most from one another is their relative performance and sophistication. But two other key factors are the cost and the time it takes to build them.

We can start by considering open-air sun drying. Sun drying merely requires a tray or rack for food that can be placed outdoors. This works fine for some applications, and there is little or no material cost involved. However sun drying is relatively slow and results are unpredictable. Food is exposed to the elements (rain, wind and dust), and constant supervision is needed to make sure raccoons don't run away with it, birds don't poop on it, mice don't munch on it, and ants, bees and flies are kept away. Placing food on a rooftop, hanging it on a line, or making an elevated drying rack like the Native Americans used to do will solve some of these problems. It works, it's just not the most convenient, efficient, secure or sanitary way to dry food. And the quality of the food may suffer if drying times are prolonged or weather changes.

The first stage in solar drying, in terms of design sophistication, is the "hot box" dryer in which the food is enclosed and protected in a box or tent with a clear covering. This design might resemble a cold frame or a miniature greenhouse. The food is now somewhat protected and the drying temperature is elevated significantly. Many people have had good results with very simple solar hot boxes. One reason these simple designs work fairly well is that the food is heated directly by the sun, boosting its temperature and driving moisture from the food into the air. But because there are no vents to let the air and moisture escape, it gets very hot and humid inside the hot box dryer. The moisture condenses on the inside of the hot box and drips down the sides or toward a drip channel.

While nice and simple, these units clearly don't perform as well as they could. The high humidity inside slows the drying process, there's little air movement, and all that condensate may rot your frame. If the weather is slightly overcast or there just isn't much sunshine, the warm, moist conditions of a hot box can cause rapid food spoilage. In addition, it may be hard to achieve the degree of dryness you need for long-term food storage. You can improve upon this design by adding venting that allows the moisture to escape and increases air movement.

The Maui Fruit Dryer

This 1976 photo shows Jeff White with the solar dryer he built and used for many years on Maui, Hawaii. It's fully loaded with home-grown bananas. The glazing was a 3-by-8-foot sheet of ¼-inch tempered glass that was sloped about 15° and fixed on a wood frame with a plywood bottom. Lots of ½"-diameter holes were drilled in the bottom and sides to assist venting. These were covered with screens. Access was through the rear hinged door. Inside were two 3-by-4-foot screen-covered frames made from two-by-fours for the food. A big load of whole (unsliced) bananas would take about four days to dry completely. Jeff and his wife Judi also dried mangoes, pineapple and papayas, which they stored in one-gallon glass jars. See Judi's delicious banana recipe in Chapter 5.

Maui Dryer

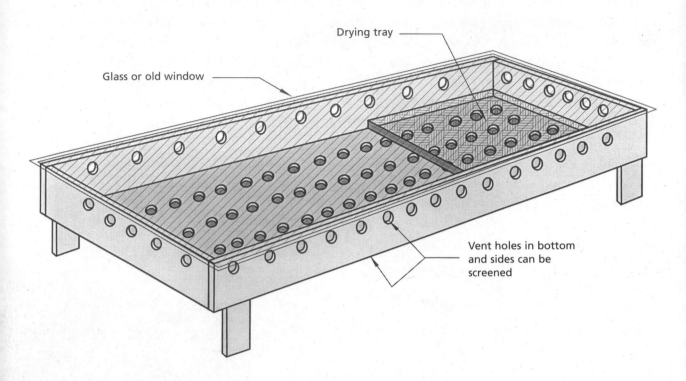

Drying tray

Glass or old window

Vent holes in bottom
and sides can be
screened

3-4: *Basic solar hot box dryer with venting*

DENNIS SCANLIN

3-5: *This solar hot box dryer uses a
PVC "chimney" to increase venting*

Typically, holes are made in the bottom and top so that the warm, moist air can rise up and exit the dryer (see Figure 3-4). All vent openings should be screened.

An adjustable vent can be added to control temperature, and an access door can be installed to facilitate loading and unloading. At this point we have a fairly sturdy structure that will dry food reasonably well and keep pests out. If you live in a hot, sunny, arid, or tropical environment, you could stop here. Otherwise, there are still significant improvements that can be made.

A good airflow path is critical to efficient drying. In the modified hot box dryer, cool air enters the dryer at the bottom, passes through the food once as it is getting warmed by the sun [and the food], and then leaves through the top vent. The air path is so short that most of the heat has escaped through the top vent and been wasted! Ideally, we want to begin heating the air as soon as it enters the dryer and *before* it reaches the food. Then we want to make all this warmed air pass across as much food as possible before it leaves. In this way we will squeeze the most drying power out of each watt of solar energy.

One approach to solar drying is to separate the two basic functions that occur in a solar dryer. One function is the solar collector that gathers the solar radiation and converts it to hot air. The other is the dryer cabinet that holds the racks of food for drying. Many of the high-performance designs are based on this strategy. The collector is tilted and placed below the cabinet so that natural convection will drive the air movement. Outside air enters at the bottom front of the collector, warms as it

Wilson Bruning with dryer

High on Drying

Wilson Bruning of John Day, Oregon, built a version of the Appalachian Dryer in 2004, and the whole family has been enjoying it ever since. Wilson scaled down the design, using half the normal glazing area and only three shelves to make the dryer smaller so it would be more portable and could fit in his car. He says it works well in his sunny, arid climate and dries most things in one day. Dried apples are his most popular product.

rises and passes through the collector, leaves the collector, and enters the dryer cabinet, where it rises up through the multiple food racks. Venting and temperature is controlled by adjusting the vent opening at the top of the cabinet.

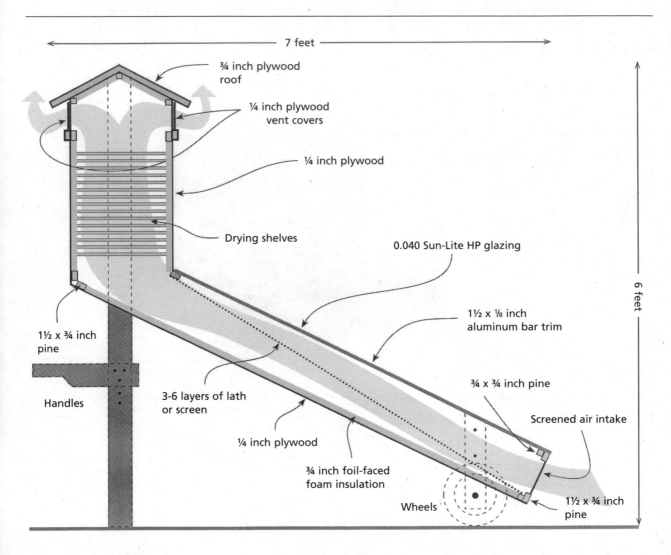

¾ inch plywood roof

¼ inch plywood vent covers

¼ inch plywood

Drying shelves

0.040 Sun-Lite HP glazing

1½ x ⅛ inch aluminum bar trim

1½ x ¾ inch pine

Handles

3-6 layers of lath or screen

¾ x ¾ inch pine

Screened air intake

¼ inch plywood

¾ inch foil-faced foam insulation

Wheels

1½ x ¾ inch pine

7 feet

6 feet

3-6: *The Appalachian Dryer combines a solar collector and dryer cabinet*
(*Illustration courtesy of* Home Power Magazine)

This two-part system is efficient and can have excellent performance, if designed properly. The Appalachian Dryer shown in Figure 3-6 is an example of one of the best designs. More information about this design can be found in the *Home Power Magazine* articles listed in the *Resources* section in Appendix E.

This type of solar dryer can accommodate a fairly large quantity of food because the trays can be stacked in the separate cabinet. Since the food is being heated indirectly by the warm air, and not directly by the sun, the total glazing area must be large enough to provide an adequate heat source. The large collector area can make the overall dryer a bit big and bulky and difficult to transport (and hard to fit in most vehicles). The Appalachian Dryer design adds wheels and handles to improve mobility.

Two other similar designs are worth mentioning. Rodale Plans developed a two-part dryer design in 1981 that can be folded up into a box (*Rodale Plans: Solar Food Dryer*, 1981, out of print). The solar collector section folds in half and is hinged to the cabinet. The legs also collapse so the entire unit takes minimum storage space. While smartly engineered, there is still some inconvenience associated with the setup and take-down. Due to its size, the entire unit probably weighs quite a bit, making it difficult to carry and move around to adjust for different sun angles during the day.

The Rodale dryer uses a down-draft design that requires the warm air to pass down through the cabinet before exiting upwards through the rear chimney section. This was probably done to allow for a longer collector and a lower cabinet height (for access). While this unit reportedly worked well, this airflow pattern could be problematic, since warm air doesn't really want to go down. The Rodale design includes a fan in the chimney section to encourage proper airflow when necessary. This design also includes a backup electric heating system consisting of four 40-watt light bulbs (160 watts total). The heater is located at the top of the dryer cabinet and is used to assist the drying when the weather is poor. The glazing area is 8 feet long by 30 inches wide and uses a flexible polyester (Mylar) film material that allowed the collector section to be folded.

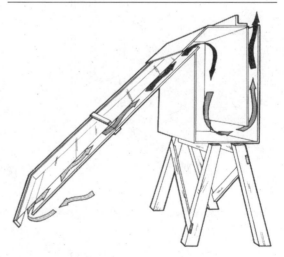

3-7: *The Rodale Plans solar dryer used a down-draft configuration*

Another noteworthy design is the New Mexico Dryer, a hybrid two-part dryer system that includes both direct and indirect solar heating. The sketches in Figure 3-8 show the front covered with a flexible fiberglass film glazing (like Sun-Lite HP fiberglass). The lower section is the solar collector with a corrugated metal absorber plate (45 inches wide and 26 inches deep). The glazing runs up and over the food trays to increase solar gain and direct heating action. Dimensions of the fiberglass sheet are 48 inches wide by 8 feet 4 inches long. This appears to be a very effective dryer design that uses direct heating and has an ample glazing area. One can

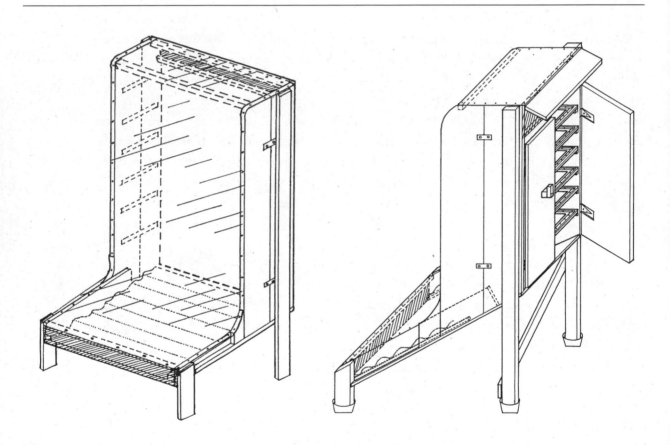

3-8: *The New Mexico solar food dryer combines direct and indirect solar heating.*
(From How to Build a Solar Crop Dryer, *undated, but circa 1980, by New Mexico Solar Energy Association.)*

imagine that the food trays would dry faster on the top and on the sunny side, but the trays could easily be rotated once a day for even drying. There's no backup heating in this design, but then you may not need one in New Mexico.

The SunWorks SFD, designed by the author, integrates the solar collector and food drying cabinet into a compact configuration that is relatively light and portable (Figure 3-9). The convenience of compact size and portability is

3-9: *The SunWorks Solar Food Dryer integrates the solar collector and drying cabinet for convenience and portability*

a significant attribute in a food dryer that will be used regularly.

The illustration in Figure 3-10 shows how the SunWorks SFD solar collector works, with the absorber plate converting solar radiation to heat. The design uses both direct heating (like the solar hot box dryer) and indirect heating from the absorber plate. The airflow in the SunWorks SFD is designed to optimize performance and achieve even drying (see Figure 3-11),

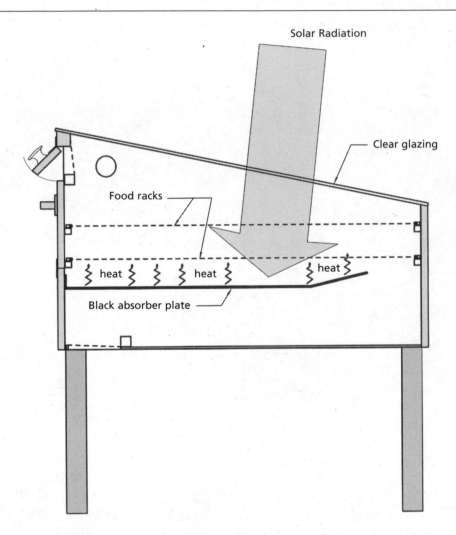

3-10: *The SunWorks SFD is an efficient solar collector*

and ventilation is powered by natural convection (the solar fan). Buoyant warm air rises and exits the upper rear vent, and cool air is drawn in through the bottom vent inlet to replace the warm air. The cool air is warmed as it flows under the absorber plate from the back to the front of the dryer. The air then rises and warms further as it flows back across the top of the absorber plate. As the warm air flows back toward the rear vents it passes over the food on both trays. This enables the warm air to remove as much moisture as possible from the food before exiting.

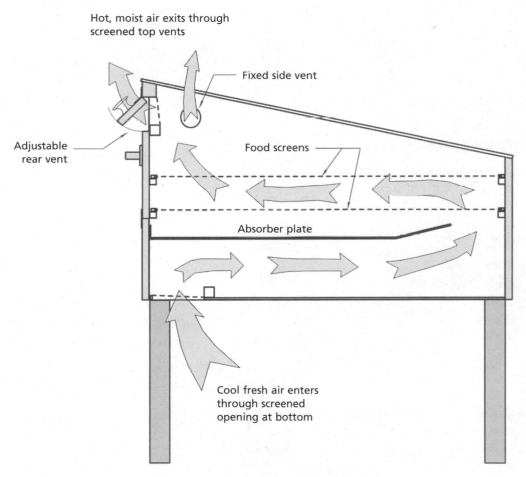

Hot, moist air exits through screened top vents

Fixed side vent

Adjustable rear vent

Food screens

Absorber plate

Cool fresh air enters through screened opening at bottom

3-11: *The air flow pattern in the SunWorks SFD is designed to maximize effectiveness*

3-12: *A built-in food dryer at Aprovecho Research Center*

The SunWorks SFD includes a 400-watt backup electric heating system that can take over when the sun goes into hiding, or in the winter when you need to do some off-season drying. The backup heating system uses the same natural convection air flow as the solar heating, so no fans are needed.

Another interesting design idea for a solar food dryer is the built-in unit that can be attached to the south side of the house and accessed through a window. The unit shown in Figure 3-12 is from the Aprovecho Research Center in Cottage Grove, Oregon. This seems like a great idea for maximizing convenience. However, there are some possible drawbacks, which may have led to this one being out of commission at the time I took this photo. First, it blocks some of your window. Then, accessing the dryer requires removing the window screen. Without a screen, you can't keep the window open for ventilation in the summer when you'll be doing the drying. If you do keep the window open while drying, unwanted heat from the dryer can come into the house (along with the insects the screen would keep out). While this configuration has some appeal, one has to consider what's gained from a design that has you spending more time indoors on a sunny day.

There are many other designs for solar food dryers that were not included here. Some of these may work well, but many were left out because they are made from cardboard, have potential design problems, or are too big and bulky for the typical home gardener.

CHAPTER 4

Complete Instructions for Making Your Own Solar Food Dryer

You can make your own SunWorks SFD (solar food dryer) with readily available materials by following the instructions in this chapter. Once you have all the materials on hand, you can build this dryer in about two days. A table saw, circular saw, fine-toothed hand saw (or jig saw), staple gun and a cordless drill (with a Phillips screwdriver bit) are all the equipment you'll need. If you lack access to a table saw, you can use a circular saw with straight-edge and get satisfactory results.

Assembly instructions refer to materials from the parts list that follows and to diagrams in the chapter. These instructions are based on using standard new materials that can be obtained almost anywhere. If you are interested in using recycled materials, see the sidebar in this chapter for tips.

SunWorks Solar Dryer Features

The SunWorks SFD is a high-performance, solar-powered food dryer that can be placed in any sunny outdoor location. It operates on 100 percent passive solar energy, but also has full backup electric heating to take over during bad weather, or for off-season (winter) operation. Solar energy heats air 60° to 100° F above ambient (outdoor) temperature. Adjustable venting allows for temperature control. Screening protects food from insects and critters.

The design is compact, portable and relatively lightweight, making it easy to use and put away. Its sturdy, weatherproof design is intended for a long life of regular use. It's assembled with screws so that any part can be repaired or replaced as necessary.

The direct-heating design speeds drying by boosting the effective temperature by about 20° F. The clear glass glazing filters most ultraviolet light and allows you to visually monitor the food without opening the unit. Two large food trays are made from lightweight aluminum frames that are easy to clean and provide capacity for up to six pounds of fresh food.

4-1: *SunWorks solar food dryer*

Tips on Using Recycled Materials

Recycled materials will generally produce excellent results and will save you quite a bit of expense and go even easier on the planet. Minor design modifications may be necessary to adjust dimensions to fit the materials available.

If you have a recycling center with building materials, look for aluminum windows and screens that are about the same size as the ones specified here (or slightly smaller). These are the highest cost item in the solar dryer, so yield the biggest savings. Old aluminum storm doors and storm windows are a good source. Damaged screens can be repaired if the aluminum frames are in good condition (see sidebar below). Wood-framed windows and screens will work too, but add weight to the dryer and may need to be replaced sooner.

Make sure glass is clear and not tinted. It doesn't need to be tempered. The glass should be about the same size as the screens or slightly larger. Double glazing is not recommended because it adds weight and isn't necessary for good dryer performance.

The metal absorber plate can be made from any sheet metal that is thin and bendable, so check scrap metal yards and recycling centers. Aluminum material is best, since it is lightweight and doesn't rust.

Scrap plywood is often available from construction sites and from your own past building projects. Stick with ½"-thick material, if possible. Thinner material (down to ⅜") will work, but is not as sturdy. T1-11 plywood siding is fine, but don't use any particle board, LP siding or similar composite material. The ¾" trim stock used here can also be made from straight, select 2x4's, if you are handy with a table saw. Recycled hardware will also work well, including handles, hinges, knobs, and latches.

Since it is unlikely that you will be able to find recycled glass and screens of the exact size specified in these plans, you will need to adapt this design to what you have. Resize the width and depth of the dryer cabinet to fit your two screens. Then add trim or plywood to the top of the cabinet to make it fit your glass. Try to adhere to all the vertical measurements outlined here, especially for internal components and vent areas.

SunWorks SFD Specifications:

- Solar glazing area (net): 5.4 ft² (0.5 m²)
- Solar heat input: 400 to 500 W (approx., summer, mid-day)
- Drying rack area: 10.1 ft² (0.94 m²) total
- Backup heating: 400 W (adjustable)
- Overall dimensions: 30" wide, 27" deep, 28½" high
- Approximate weight: 35 lbs.

Replacing and repairing screens

Torn or damaged screens can be fixed easily if the aluminum frame is still in good shape. New polypropylene screen material will cost about $5 to $10 per screen. You'll want to replace the rubber spline as well, unless the screen is fairly new. The spline is the beading that holds the screen in the channel that runs around the frame. Be sure to get the same diameter spline as the original to assure a snug fit. Use a plastic-wheeled spline tool to make this easier (metal-wheeled tools can cut the screen). Cut the screen mesh so that it is about an inch larger than the frame on all sides. Lay the frame on a table or floor. Place the screen over the frame and use the spline tool to gently push the screen into the channel along one side. Then place the spline over the channel and push it in with the notched roller on the spline tool. Work around the frame until you are back at the beginning. If the screen isn't taut enough, pull out one side, tighten and replace the spline. Don't overtighten screens or you will warp the frame. When done, cut the extra spline off and trim the screen with a utility knife.

Assembly Instructions

Before you begin, order the glazing and screens from a local window or glass shop based on the following specifications:

Glazing: ⅛-inch-thick clear window glass framed with aluminum trim to protect the glass (and you). Aluminum trim should be about ½ inch wide and about ¼ inch thick. Final outside dimensions are 27¾ inches by 30 inches.

Screens: Two screens of 25½ inches by 28½ inches (outside dimensions) with mill-finish (uncoated) aluminum frames and fiberglass screen material. Charcoal-colored screen is better than gray because the darker color absorbs more solar energy. (Note: It's possible to make your own screens for a slight savings by purchasing screen kits from the hardware store and cutting them to the correct size.)

Food-Safe Screens: If you want to be able to place food directly on FDA-approved, food-safe screens without using any inserts, use a polypropylene screen material. You will need two 27-by-30-inch pieces of screen (see *Resources* in Appendix E for sources).

Parts List for the SunWorks Solar Food Dryer

This list will help you gather everything you need to build your dryer. If it is unclear what any of these parts look like, check the assembly photos before purchasing them.

Materials

- Plywood for cabinet sides, ½" thick, 4' x 4' sheet, AC exterior grade
- Wood paneling for bottom panel, 22" x 29" and ⅛" thick or lauan door skin material (thicker material is okay, but adds weight)
- Cedar legs and top rear brace from 10'-length of cedar 2 x 2 (1½" x 1½")
- Wood rack supports and misc. parts: 10 pieces, ¾" x ¾" trim material, totalling 236" (about 20'), or cut from select 2 x 4 – 8' KD (dried wood)
- Wood rack supports: 2 pieces ¾" x ½" trim material, totalling 52", or cut from above 2 x 4
- Sheet metal for metal heat plate: 31" x 23" (use 0.025"thick aluminum or galvanized sheet metal that is thin enough to be bent by hand)
- Rubber or closed-cell foam weatherstrip (adhesive on one side) for glazing seal, 10' length, approx. ½" wide by ¼" thick

- Screen material for vents: 24" by 30" fiberglass window screen

Hardware

- Access door hinges: 2 triangular, standard, 1" wide by 2" (or similar)
- Access door latch: swinging latch (safety hasp)
- Access door handle: 4½" basic-style brass
- Vent door hinges: 2 standard, square, 1½" wide by ¾" (or similar)
- Vent door knobs: 2 wood pull knobs
- Vent door friction support (lid support for adjusting vent)
- Side carrying handles: two 5½" basic handles
- Glazing mounting brackets: six 2" by ½" metal plates (bendable steel)
- Corner braces: two 1" x ½" metal angles (L-shaped)
- Light fixtures for heating bulbs: two Leviton porcelain surface mounting sockets (or similar)
- Electric wire: 5' of 16-gauge lamp cord (brown or black)
- Electrical lamp plug (two-prong)
- Light bulbs: two 200-watt utility bulbs (incandescent, not fluorescent)
- 50 screws, size 6, 1¼" flat head, zinc coated
- 25 screws, size 6, 1" flat head, zinc coated
- 20 screws, size 6, ¾" flat head, zinc coated
- 25 screws, size 6, ½" flat head, zinc coated
- 25 screws, size 6, ½" pan head, zinc coated

4-2: *Porcelain fixture for backup heating*

4-3: *Stem-type thermometer*

- Thermometer: Bi-metal, stem-type with 2″ dial and 0-220° F range, such as the Taylor model 6215 (see *Resources* in Appendix E).

Other supplies:

- Spray paint for absorber plate: flat black, high-temperature stove paint (such as Stovebrite)
- Fine sandpaper to prep aluminum sheet metal for painting
- Reflective aluminum metal tape, about 2″ width

Step 1

Make the absorber plate first, since you will want the paint to be dry before installation. Cut aluminum or galvanized sheet material to dimensions indicated on the Absorber Plate Diagram. Clean metal to remove any oils or films. Lightly sand the entire surface of both sides to help the paint adhere better. Drill and fold material as shown in diagram. Place on drop cloth and paint with flat black paint suitable for high temperature applications (like barbeques and stove pipes). Apply two light coats. When dry, flip over and paint other side. Let dry completely before installing.

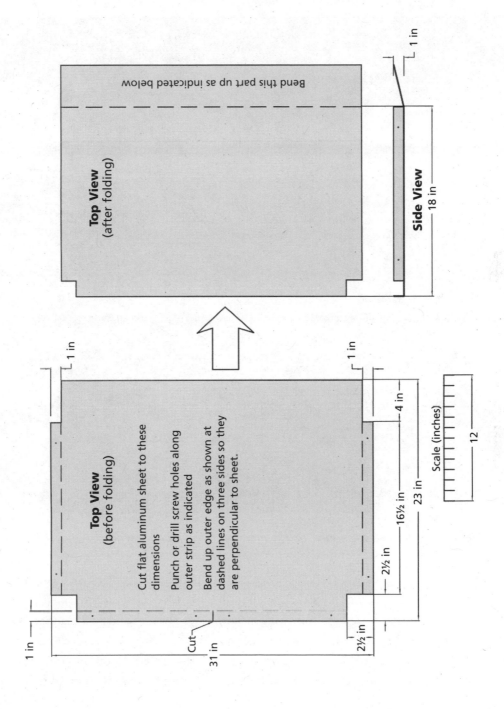

SunWorks SFD Absorber Plate Diagram

Top View
(after folding)

Bend this part up as indicated below

Side View

18 in

1 in

Top View
(before folding)

Cut flat aluminum sheet to these dimensions

Punch or drill screw holes along outer strip as indicated

Bend up outer edge as shown at dashed lines on three sides so they are perpendicular to sheet.

Cut

1 in

31 in

4 in

2½ in

16½ in

23 in

2½ in

1 in

Scale (inches)

12

4-4: *Clamp a straight piece of wood on the metal to make a good bend*

Step 2

Cut all plywood cabinet pieces as shown in the Plywood Cutting Diagram. Make sure material is flat and right-angle corners are square. For best appearance, orient the plywood so that the grain on the good (finished) side appears as indicated on the diagram. (Tip: If you don't have a pickup truck or roof rack to haul the plywood sheet, you can have the first cut made at most lumber/hardware stores so that it's easier to transport.) Make the angled cut on the side panels with a circular saw by clamping a straightedge to the plywood.

SunWorks SFD Plywood Cutting Diagram

4' x 4' sheet, ½ inch, AC exterior grade

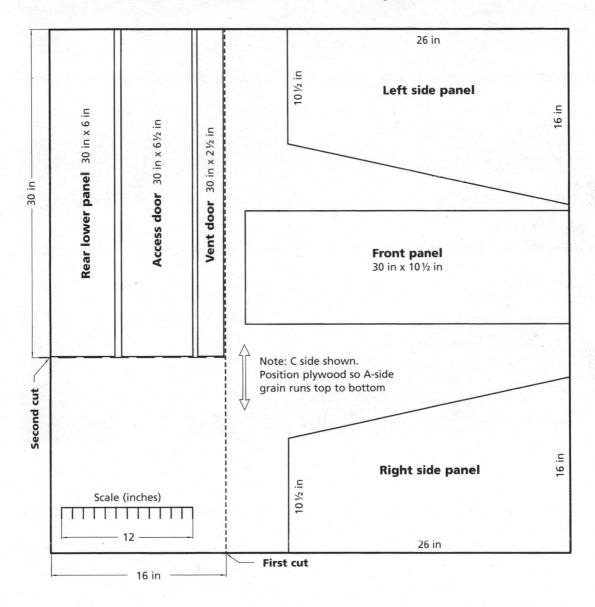

30 in

Rear lower panel 30 in x 6 in

Access door 30 in x 6½ in

Vent door 30 in x 2½ in

26 in

10½ in

Left side panel

16 in

Front panel
30 in x 10½ in

Note: C side shown.
Position plywood so A-side
grain runs top to bottom

Second cut

Scale (inches)

12

10½ in

Right side panel

16 in

26 in

First cut

16 in

4-5: *Making the angled cut*

Step 3

Make all "special cuts" as shown on the Special Cuts Diagram. Take extra care to make sure the notch in the top corner of each of the side panels is measured and marked properly before cutting. Use a jig saw or fine-toothed hand saw to get a good, clean cut (see Figure 4-6).

After cutting the top rear brace, check to make sure it fits snugly in the notch you just made in the side panels. The top bevel should match the top slope of the side panels. Adjust fit if necessary.

SunWorks SFD   Special Cuts Diagram

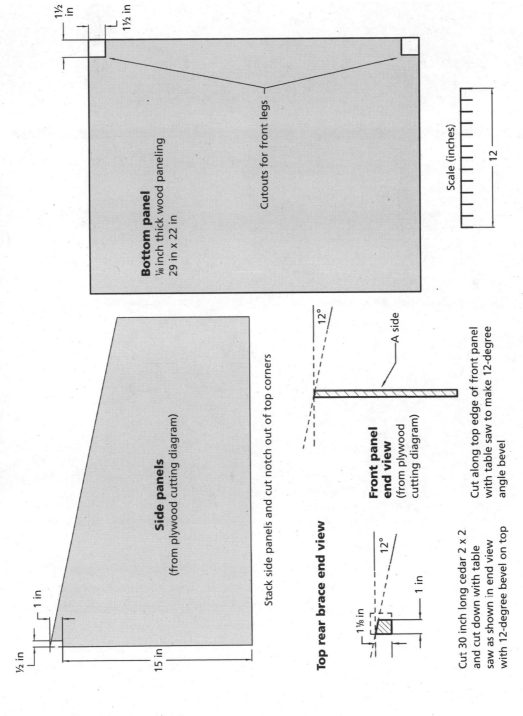

Bottom panel
⅛ inch thick wood paneling
29 in x 22 in

Cutouts for front legs

1½ in

1½ in

Scale (inches)

12

Side panels
(from plywood cutting diagram)

Stack side panels and cut notch out of top corners

1 in

15 in

½ in

Front panel end view
(from plywood cutting diagram)

12°

A side

Cut along top edge of front panel with table saw to make 12-degree angle bevel

Top rear brace end view

12°

1 in

1⅛ in

Cut 30 inch long cedar 2 x 2 and cut down with table saw as shown in end view with 12-degree bevel on top

4-6: *A jig saw works well for this corner cutout*

The bottom panel should be as square as possible, since it will set the shape for the cabinet. Use actual measurements for the leg cutouts if your legs are not close to the 1½-by-1½-inch dimensions shown.

Make all "miscellaneous cuts" shown on the Misc. Cuts Diagram. You can save a few bucks by using a table saw to rip-cut the ¾-by-¾-inch and ½-by-¾-inch pieces from one good 8-foot two-by-four.

SunWorks SFD Miscellaneous Cuts Diagram

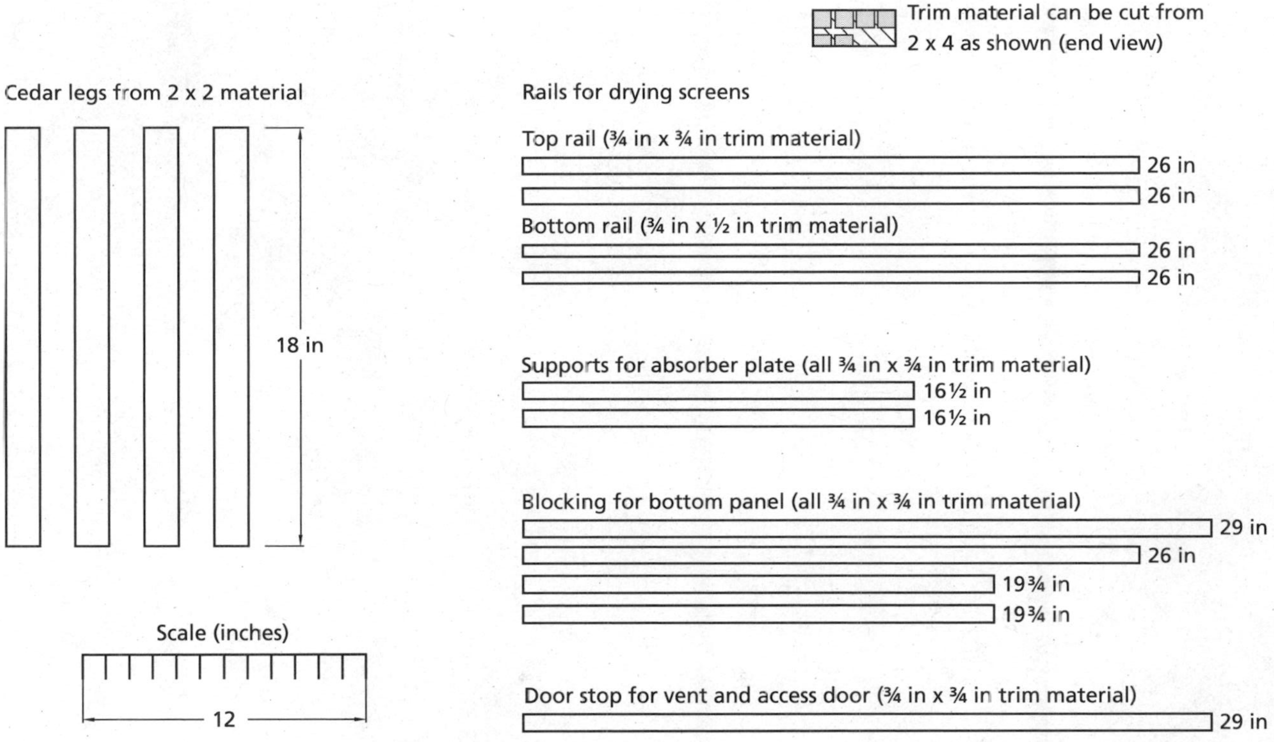

Trim material can be cut from 2 x 4 as shown (end view)

Rails for drying screens

Top rail (¾ in x ¾ in trim material)

26 in

26 in

Bottom rail (¾ in x ½ in trim material)

26 in

26 in

Supports for absorber plate (all ¾ in x ¾ in trim material)

16½ in

16½ in

Blocking for bottom panel (all ¾ in x ¾ in trim material)

29 in

26 in

19¾ in

19¾ in

Door stop for vent and access door (¾ in x ¾ in trim material)

29 in

Cedar legs from 2 x 2 material

18 in

Scale (inches)

12

You have now cut all the wood pieces and are now ready to start assembly.

Step 4

Fasten legs onto side panels as shown in Assembly Diagram #1 with two 1¼-inch screws. Keep legs square and flush with the sides of the panel. Set all legs to extend 12 inches from bottom of side panel. Pre-drilling and countersinking screw holes in the plywood (but not the legs) will give the best result.

Step 5

Install shelf rails and supports (made in Step 3) on the inside of both side panels with 1-inch screws as shown in Assembly

4-7: Attach legs to side panels

4-8: Rails on inside of side panels

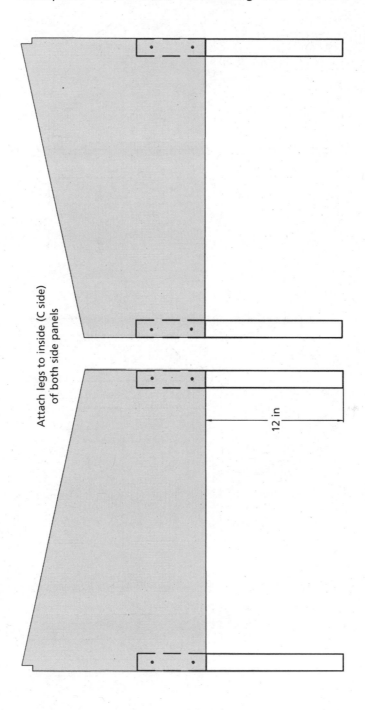

SunWorks SFD   Assembly Diagram #1

Attach legs to inside (C side) of both side panels

12 in

SunWorks SFD Assembly Diagram #2

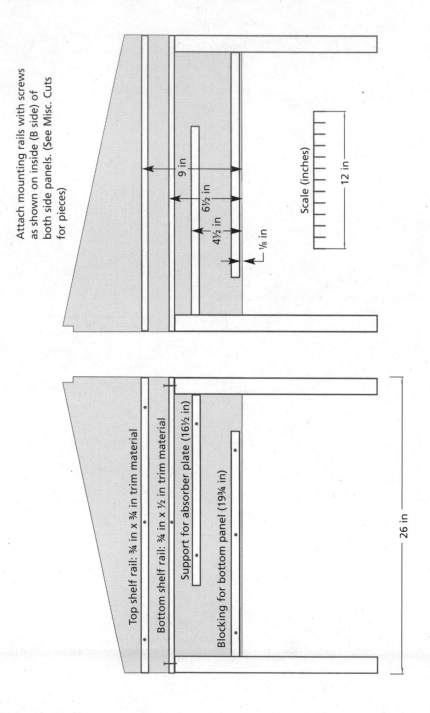

Attach mounting rails with screws as shown on inside (B side) of both side panels. (See Misc. Cuts for pieces)

9 in

6½ in

4½ in

⅛ in

Scale (inches)

12 in

Top shelf rail: ¾ in x ¾ in trim material

Bottom shelf rail: ¾ in x ½ in trim material

Support for absorber plate (16½ in)

Blocking for bottom panel (19¾ in)

26 in

Diagram #2. To avoid cracking the wood, pre-drill and countersink holes in rails/supports (but not the plywood).

Step 6

Complete cabinet box by installing front and rear panels as shown in Assembly Diagram #3. Make sure ends of front and rear panels are flush with the side panels before attaching with 1¼-inch screws into the legs.

4-9: *Cabinet box*

SunWorks SFD
Assembly Diagram #3

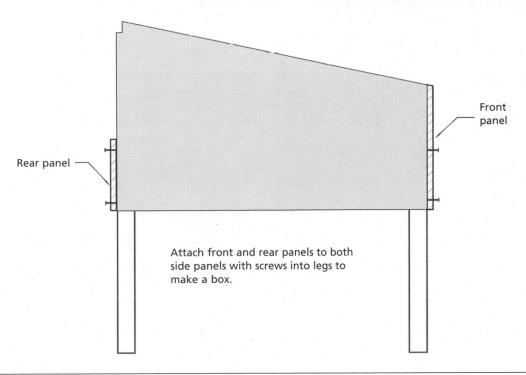

Front panel

Rear panel

Attach front and rear panels to both side panels with screws into legs to make a box.

Step 7 (Optional Electric Backup Heating System)

Note: It is recommended that you confirm that this procedure complies with your local electrical code. If you are not sure how to properly wire these fixtures, get help from someone who does!

Install utility light fixtures on inside of the rear panel as shown in Assembly Diagram #4. Be sure to set the screws in the porcelain fixtures by hand (instead of with a drill) to avoid cracking the fixtures. Wire with 16-gauge lamp wire

to make backup heating system as shown in the Wiring Diagram. Drill a small hole in either of the side panels for the wire. Run the wire through the hole, but tie a knot in the wire first so that the knot takes any tension that might be put on the cord from outside the unit. Leave a small amount of slack in the cord inside.

Cut the electric cord about 12 inches from the outside of the box and install a plug on the end. The final result should leave the plug hanging an inch or two above ground level. This

SunWorks SFD   Assembly Diagram #4

Install backup heating

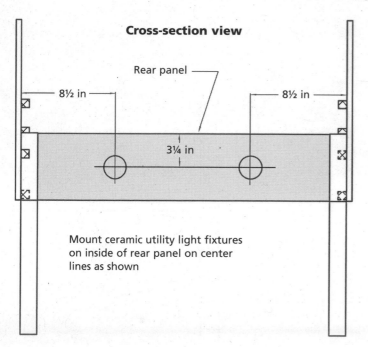

Cross-section view

Rear panel

8½ in

8½ in

3¼ in

Mount ceramic utility light fixtures on inside of rear panel on center lines as shown

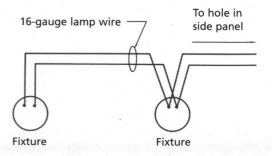

Wiring diagram

Wire with 5-foot length of 16-gauge lamp wire

16-gauge lamp wire

To hole in side panel

Fixture

Fixture

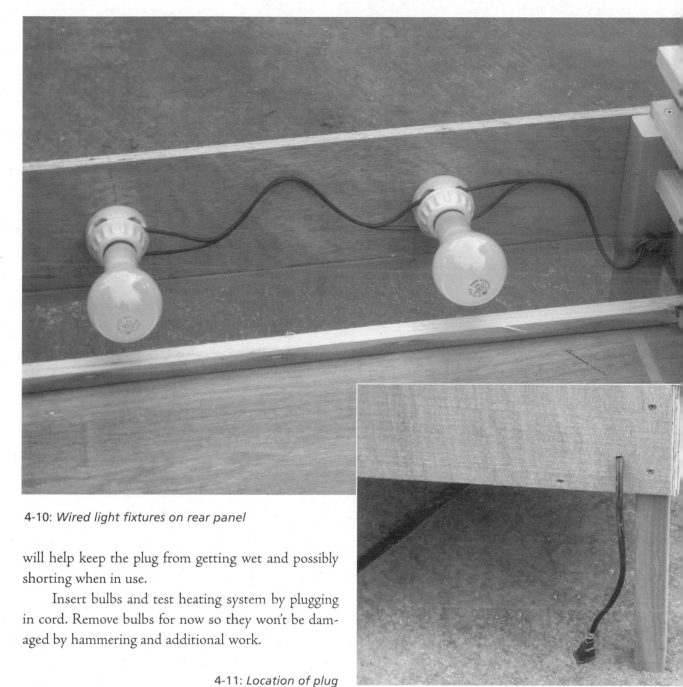

4-10: *Wired light fixtures on rear panel*

will help keep the plug from getting wet and possibly shorting when in use.

Insert bulbs and test heating system by plugging in cord. Remove bulbs for now so they won't be damaged by hammering and additional work.

4-11: *Location of plug*

Step 8

Using Assembly Diagram #5, and also referring to Assembly Diagram #6, install the following parts:

1. Drill 1½-inch diameter vent holes on each side of dryer with a hole-saw bit in location shown on Diagram #5. (These holes maintain a minimum amount of venting at all times.)

2. Drill thermometer insertion hole as shown on Diagram #5 (use ⅛-inch bit, or same size as your thermometer stem).

SunWorks SFD   Assembly Diagram #5

Complete Side View Cut Away

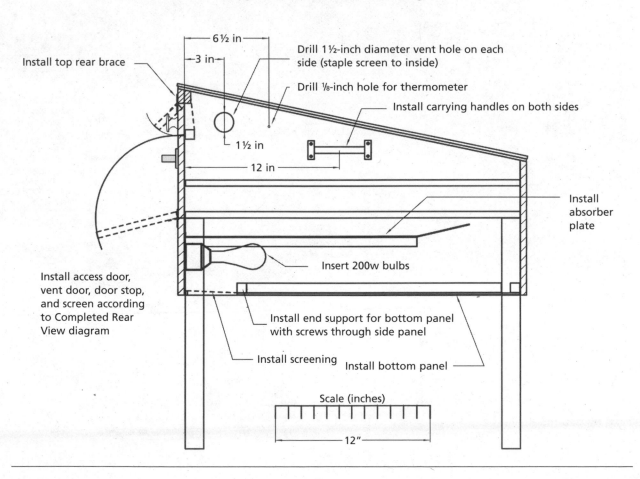

Install top rear brace

6 ½ in

3 in

Drill 1 ½-inch diameter vent hole on each side (staple screen to inside)

Drill ⅛-inch hole for thermometer

Install carrying handles on both sides

1 ½ in

12 in

Install absorber plate

Install access door, vent door, door stop, and screen according to Completed Rear View diagram

Insert 200w bulbs

Install end support for bottom panel with screws through side panel

Install screening

Install bottom panel

Scale (inches)

12"

3. Install end support for bottom panel. Fasten by screwing 1¼-inch screw through each side panel.

4. Cut screen for bottom vent about one inch larger on all sides than vent area. Staple screen onto bottom of end support (from step 8-3 above) and then to sides, legs and back of cabinet. Use a thin strip of wood to get a good bug-proof seal along the back (about ⅛ by ½ by 26 inches). Staple this strip over the screen.

5. Install the bottom panel with ½-inch pan-head screws. Pre-drilling screw holes in the panel will improve strength. The bottom

SunWorks SFD   Assembly Diagram #6

Complete Rear View (see through)

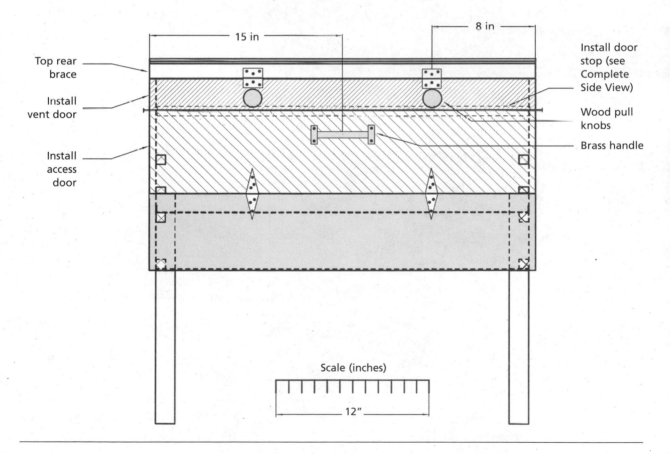

Top rear brace

Install vent door

Install access door

15 in

8 in

Install door stop (see Complete Side View)

Wood pull knobs

Brass handle

Scale (inches)

12"

4-12: *Drill vent holes.*

4-13: *Attaching bottom screen*

panel should be used to make the cabinet square, so check corners and adjust cabinet as necessary.

6. Apply several rows of aluminum tape to cover the wood end support (for bottom panel) and the bottom panel below light bulbs to protect these from heat and to reflect light up to absorber plate.

7. Install the absorber plate using ½-inch pan-head screws. To get the plate in, you will need to insert one side and then gently bend the plate in the middle to get the other side in. To facilitate bending the metal, make a one-inch vertical cut in the middle of the rear fastening strip (the part that is folded up), as shown in the Absorber Plate Diagram. After the plate is in place, straighten out and adjust or re-bend front section as necessary.

8. Install the two 200-watt utility light bulbs by reaching under the absorber plate. You can use a lower wattage bulb if desired. From this point on, avoid dropping or banging unit (i.e., with a hammer), as this can damage the filaments in the bulbs. (Note: To replace bulbs in the future, remove either the glazing or the bottom panel, whichever is easier.)

4-14: *Install bottom panel*

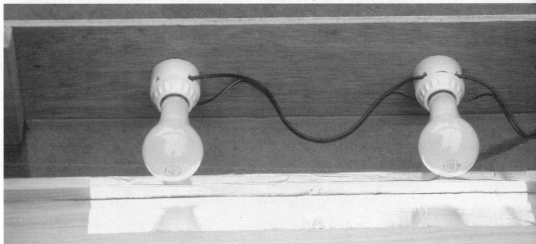

4-15: *Apply aluminum tape to wood below bulbs*

4-16: *Attach top rear brace*

9. Install carrying handles on both sides. These should be placed at the center of gravity so that the unit is balanced (i.e., not in the center of the side panel). Use the locational dimensions given in the diagram. If you are using different materials or dimensions than those specified here, wait until your unit is completed and then install handles at the best location for balance.

10. Install the top rear brace (from the Special Cuts Diagram) using L-shaped corner braces on each end to attach it to the side panels.

11. Install the vent door screen by stapling the screen to the bottom of the doorstop, wrapping it around the front of the doorstop and going up to the front side of the top rear brace. Staple the top edge of the screen along the top of the brace where it will be covered by the weather-strip and glazing. Staple the sides of the screen to the inside of the side panels. Trim off extra screen with scissors.

12. Cut two 3-by-3-inch squares of screen and staple on the inside of 1½-inch fixed vent holes in side panels.

Step 9

Using Assembly Diagram #6, and also referring back to Diagram #5 for additional reference, install the following parts:

1. Install triangular access-door hinges on bottom panel and then attach access door.

2. Install square vent-door hinges on top rear brace and then attach vent door.

3. Check fit between doors and adjust as necessary to get a good, close fit that allows both doors to operate smoothly. This may require removing both doors and cutting away some of the inside edges with a table saw or plane so each door can swing freely.

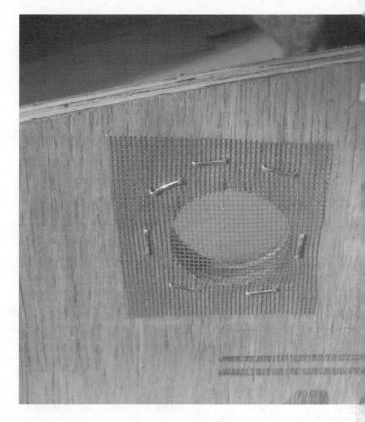

4-17: *Screen side vents*

4. Attach handle on access door.

5. Attach wood pull knobs on vent door.

6. Install friction lid support to control vent door opening. Make sure that the slider functions from full open to full closed position before fastening in place. Depending on the model, you may need to unscrew the friction adjusting screw and flip the slider over to fit properly.

7. Install latch on access door. Latch should keep door firmly shut.

4-18: *Attach rear hardware*

4-19: *Friction lid support*

4-20: *Access door latch*

Step 10

Your dryer is now ready for the final step — installing the glazing. First, clean out all sawdust and debris from inside the cabinet with a brush and vacuum.

Place ½-inch-wide foam weatherstripping along top edge of cabinet frame where the window will rest (adhesive side down). Align weatherstrip with the outside edge of cabinet. If necessary, secure weatherstrip by stapling near corners and centers along the inside edge.

Place glazing on dryer in the proper position. Use the glazing mounting brackets (2-by-½-inch metal plates) to hold the glazing in position. Custom bend the top ½ inch of each bracket to match the angle of the glazing. Bend bracket by placing it in a table vice and adjusting it with pliers and a hammer. Place brackets around frame: two in front, one on each side and two in back. Secure brackets to the sides of the cabinet with ½-inch flat head screws. Brackets should be snug, but shouldn't force glazing downward, as the weight of the glass will assure a good seal. The mounting brackets should leave a gap to allow the glass (and aluminum frame) to have room for ⅛-inch thermal expansion in both directions.

Step 11

Congratulations! Your solar food dryer is now complete. Slide in the screens, insert your ther-mometer, put it in the sun and watch it heat up!

Before using your dryer with food, place it in the sun with the vent door closed for a full day to completely dry the absorber paint and remove any moisture in the wood. Wash screens thoroughly, but gently, with dish soap and water to remove any manufacturing residues.

Enhancements

The wood exterior of the dryer can be finished with linseed oil or paint, if desired.

Add casters to the legs for mobility.

Boost performance by 10°F during extended season operation (when sun angles are low) by making the inside of the access door reflective. The aluminum tape (used above) works well for this.

For design updates and more ideas for using and enhancing your Sunworks SFD, go to: www.solarfooddryer.com.

4-21: *Custom bend brackets to fit glazing (A-front, B-rear, C-side)*

4-22: Completed dryer

CHAPTER 5

Putting Your Solar Dryer to Work

What to Dry

While virtually all foods can be dried, some are definitely better than others. The flavor of some foods, like tomatoes, bananas, and mushrooms, improves with drying. Others, like cucumbers and salad greens, are simply best when fresh. I encourage you to experiment. To get you started, I've listed some of the best sure-fire bets for drying in Table 5-1.

Food Preparation for Drying

To achieve the best results, you'll want the food to dry quickly and evenly. To do this, slice food to an even thickness of about ¼ inch. Slice foods so that the skin is cut and the flesh is exposed as much as possible.

The skin of fruits and vegetables is there for a purpose: It seals in the moisture of the food as it grows and ripens under the hot sun. This same skin can prevent your food from

Table 5-1: Food Drying Favorites	
Fruits	**Vegetables**
apples	broccoli
apricots	carrots
bananas	cauliflower
blueberries	corn
figs	green beans
grapes (seedless)	onions
peaches	peas (sweet, in pod)
pears	peppers (all types)
plums	potatoes
strawberries	tomatoes
	zucchini and summer squash
	mushrooms and herbs are excellent too!

drying quickly. Grapes, for example, have remarkably hardy skins. If uncut, grapes can sit in your dryer for several days without any apparent change. Most skins can be left on, and actually contain many of the valuable nutrients. But cutting through the skin to expose the flesh is essential for speedy drying. Apple skins can be a bit tough when dried, so peeling apples is recommended. This is easy with an old-fashioned

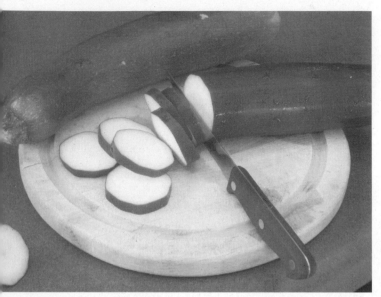

5-1: *Slicing zucchini*

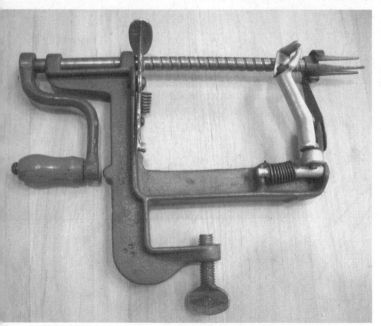

5-2: *The antique apple slicer is a food-drying essential*

5-3: *The apple slicer works well on Asian pears too*

apple slicer-peeler-corer. These devices are a food-drying essential. They are available in some specialty kitchen supply stores for around $25, and they really work (see *Resources* in Appendix E). They peel, slice and core apples in one quick operation. The resulting accordion-like apple can be sliced once more with a knife from top to bottom to yield a dozen or so perfectly round slices. The apple peeler works well with pears too, as long as they are firm and not too ripe.

Once you've prepared the food, distribute it evenly on the dryer screens and leave room around each slice for ample air movement. The SunWorks SFD uses two large drying screens, each able to hold up to three pounds of food. Overloading screens could cause them to sag and pop out of the spline. If you do need to fix or replace a screen, see the sidebar on this topic in Chapter 4.

To facilitate even drying, rotate shelves 180° and switch upper and lower shelves once about halfway through the drying process.

When to Dry

In deciding when to dry, focus on the current day's weather (or the day you plan to start drying). If it's looking mostly sunny,

go for it! Weather forecasts are too often wrong to forego drying due to a predicted chance of rain a day or two away. As long as you get a good start with drying on the first day, your food should turn out fine. If clouds or rain do come, just switch to electric backup and finish off your load that way.

You will have the potential for 10 to 14 hours a day of sunshine throughout the six months of the main food drying season (May to October). Shade cast by trees and buildings may limit sunshine in the early morning and then again late in the day. Realistically, the first and last hours of sunshine in the day do

5-4: *Spacing apples on the dryer racks (with grapes below)*

not provide much fuel for your dryer anyway, since the sun angle is so low. Eight to ten consecutive hours of good sunshine are plenty to completely dry many foods in one day. Foods with a high moisture content will take longer, but even they should get mostly dry in the first day and completely dry during the second.

At night, the temperature drops and the relative humidity of the air increases. If you are not using electric backup heating and the vents on your dryer are left open, the food can get slightly rehydrated by the moisture in the air. To keep this from happening, simply close the vents at night. If you are using electric backup, keep the vents set according to your desired temperature and be sure to turn it off the next morning before the sun is up in the sky.

How about when it's cold outside? I generally set a lower threshold of about 50° F (10° C) for reasonably fast solar drying, but it may be possible to dry at lower temperatures. You could probably still dry food when it's below freezing, but it will take many days. This has to do with the ΔT of the dryer, as explained in Chapter 3. During the low sun angles of winter, your dryer can heat air about 60° F (15.5° C) above ambient temperature (ΔT=60° F), so when it's only 32° F outside, it will be only 92° F inside the dryer. This is just not warm enough to dry food quickly. I have managed to dry foods with the SunWorks SFD in February and March in Oregon (44° north latitude) without backup electric heat. But due to the extended drying time (three to four days), the quality is not the best.

Backup Heating During Poor Weather

If the weather changes and your sunshine disappears during your first day of drying, you should consider using the electric backup heating that evening to speed the drying process along. While mostly-dried foods will handle a night in the dryer just fine, if the food is still pretty wet, the quality can be affected by this idle time. The electric backup heating system on the SunWorks SFD is just as efficient as the all-electric dryers, so don't hesitate to use it as an electric dryer during bad weather or throughout the winter months. Operating the electric heating during an overcast or rainy day is fine, but turn it off once the sun comes back out, otherwise you will have twice as much heat as you need in your dryer, which can cook or even burn your food. If you won't be around to monitor conditions, place the dryer in a shady spot before turning on the electric heating. Always plug your dryer into a GFI (ground fault interrupter) protected electrical outlet.

Operating Tips

There are a few tips for getting the most out of your solar food dryer. The first is to keep your glazing clean. A little dust or pollen on your glazing can reflect or absorb sunshine, preventing it from heating your dryer properly. If you plan to set up your dryer and leave it in one place all day, then find a location free of shading and aim the dryer due south. If you have the opportunity to check on it a few times during the day, adjust the position to track the sun. This will increase solar gain and speed drying.

When a big load of fresh food is placed in the dryer, the food warms up and a lot of moisture is released in the first few hours. Initially, condensate may form on the glazing. This is not a major concern, but opening the vent will help release the moisture. Once the condensate has cleared, close the vent a bit. When your food is almost dry and you want to drive the last bit of moisture out, close the vents enough to let the dryer temperature increase by 10 to 20 degrees for a few hours.

How Drying Preserves Food

Food preservation is essentially the process of suspending, slowing, or stopping the deterioration of food. This is accomplished primarily by arresting the growth of micro-organisms. Food spoilage occurs when bacteria, molds, or yeast have grown to such an extent that the food is rendered unpalatable, unattractive, or simply unsafe to eat. At this point, the food's nutritional value becomes irrelevant. Of course, food spoilage can also be caused by poor handling and storage, such as accidental freezing, crushing, or overheating. Freezer burn, for example, can ruin food by rendering it tasteless and unappealing.

Drying preserves food in several ways. Most importantly, drying removes water that is an essential element of all living organisms. Without water, bacteria, molds, and yeasts cannot continue to grow and damage your food. Think about life on Mars: No water, no life. Now that scientists have confirmed that water does (or did) exist on Mars, the possibility of life there exists. The drier your food, the longer it can be preserved.

Drying also works by concentrating the natural acids and sugars in your food, creating natural food preservatives. Concentrated acids and sugars, particularly abundant in fruits, create an inhospitable environment for organisms and prevent their growth. They work in the same way that salting works to preserve meat: Through osmotic pressure. Micro-organisms are destroyed or incapacitated by the osmotic pressure of concentrated salt, sugar or acid drawing moisture out of the organism's cell membrane. We are not harmed by these natural preservatives because we are a much larger organism. The preservative ingredients are diluted by the liquids we drink and other foods we eat and by the relative size of our bodies.

Heat also plays a role in preserving food. Drying at temperatures of 150° F (65° C) or higher can pasteurize food, destroying all pathogenic microorganisms. With sufficient sunshine, a good solar dryer can readily achieve temperatures high enough to pasteurize food. This may be desirable if you are drying meats or fish, or if you wish to pasteurize your food for any reason.

Drying Times and Temperatures

The warmer food gets, the faster it dries. Faster drying helps preserve nutrients and yields better flavor and better looking results. For speedy drying, I keep the temperature in the 120° to 150° F (48° to 66° C) range. I find that this works well for all fruits and vegetables. (Note that if your thermometer stem is in the sun, as with the SunWorks dryer, you will be reading the "sol-air" temperature, which is the effective temperature the food is experiencing under direct sunlight.) I don't worry too much about specific temperatures, and get consistently great results — food that looks and tastes great. The minor problems I have had mostly result from either too low a temperature due to clouds, or too high a temperature due to closed vents. Low temperatures make food dry slowly, and it may get overripe or even slightly spoiled. High temperatures can cook food and can caramelize fruits.

Temperatures of 120° F (48° C) or higher will destroy the enzymes in the food. Enzymes cause fruit to ripen. They also act to break down foods after they are harvested, causing eventual spoilage. Destroying enzymes helps with the food preservation process and prevents darkening of fruits. However, enzymes also have a role in food nutrition. Naturally occurring enzymes in foods help your digestive system break down food, which results in getting more nutrient value from the food: Hence the interest in raw foods. Folks who want to preserve all the natural raw food enzymes in their fruits and vegetables will want to dry in the 100° to 110° F (37° to 43° C) range. Drying times will be longer at lower temperatures, so there may be some tradeoffs as additional loss of vitamin C and other nutrients can occur. Herbs should also be dried at lower temperatures, in the 100° to 110° F range, to help preserve the volatile aromatic oils that contribute much of the flavors.

Drying time depends partly on the moisture content of the food and on how the food is prepared. Slicing food thinner will speed up drying. Moisture migrates through most foods fairly slowly because it has to move through many cell membranes to reach the surface. This results in practical limits to how fast you can dry certain foods. If you try to dry them too quickly, you will end up with a very dry outer layer around a wet inner core. Some people refer to this as "case hardening," but it's simply an indication that the food needs more time to dry.

How Dry is Dry Enough?

How dry you make your food is largely a matter of personal preference, but there are some general guidelines. Fruits should be dried to the point of being leathery, but not hard or brittle. Vegetables, on the other hand, should be thoroughly dried to the point of being brittle. Tomatoes can go either way, but I prefer to have them thoroughly dried for maximum storage life. Herbs should be completely dry and crumbly.

If you're not sure about the right level of dryness, err on the drier side. I find that drier is better for most foods because they hold up longer and keep their flavor better. However, if you are planning to eat the food fairly soon, some additional moisture will make them easier to rehydrate, and a bit more palatable if eaten dry.

Once your solar drying is finished, place the dried food in a sealed container and leave it on the countertop for two to three days to allow the dryness to equalize. Some pieces may be dryer than others so this step helps to distribute any remaining moisture evenly. If you find that the food is not dry enough, put it back in the dryer. Your food is now ready to be used or stored.

Storing Dried Foods

Protect the high quality and longevity of your dried produce by storing it properly. Airtight glass jars are the preferred storage containers, but plastic containers and sturdy plastic sealable bags work well too. Most importantly, always keep stored foods in a cool place (i.e., not on top of the refrigerator, in the attic, or near any heat source).

The oxygen in air is another ingredient, like water, that is essential to most life forms. Removing any extra air from the food storage containers will extend the shelf life of your dried foods and will also help preserve nutrients. Vacuum sealing and shrink wrapping are two good methods for removing extra oxygen.

While storing foods in the dark seems prudent, the adverse effect of light on stored food may have been overstated in the past. A 1997 study reported in *International Journal of Food Science* found that there was no difference in the nutrient content between jars of berry jam stored in ambient light for 13 months and those stored in the dark (*A study of some important vitamins and antioxidants in blackcurrant jam with low sugar content and without additives*, International Journal of Food Sciences and Nutrition, No. 48, pp. 57-66).

5-5: *Tomatoes drying on racks*

Many dried foods can last for up to a year without any refrigeration. Some very dry foods can last even longer. The life of dried foods can be extended further by sealing and freezing them until needed. Shrink wrapping will help reduce damage from freezer burn.

Nutrition and Food Quality

Eating freshly picked food from the garden is an optimal scenario for maximizing nutrition and flavor. However, it's far more common that some form of food storage will occur until the food is needed. Freshly picked foods may end

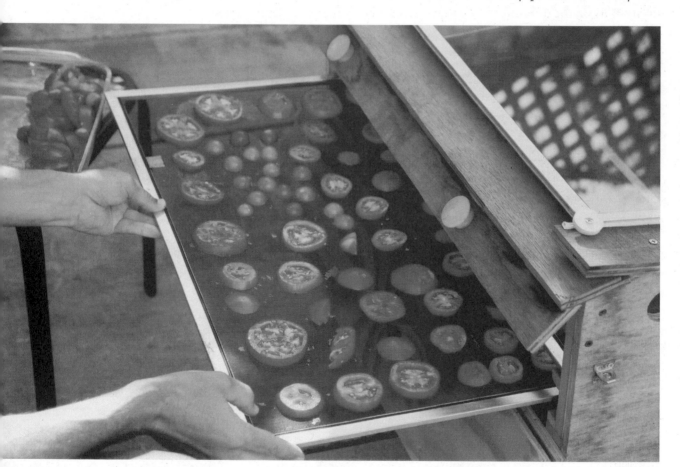

5-6: *Samples of fresh tomatoes can vary by two-fold in their content of beta-carotene (vitamin A) and vitamin C. Most organic gardeners are aware of this and strive for higher nutritional value in their produce through fertile soils and by harvesting foods in their prime. Food drying offers a method for preserving this high-quality produce well beyond the harvest season*

up sitting on farm trucks, grocery vegetable stands, kitchen countertops or in refrigerators for many days before being eaten. Extended storage can put formerly fresh food on the verge of spoiling. Poor or lengthy storage of raw foods can affect nutritional content as much as anything else. Once food has lost its flavor, begins to spoil, or looks deteriorated, we toss it out, and its nutritional value is effectively zero.

Maintaining high food quality is a primary goal in the food preservation process. Clearly you want to preserve as much of the flavor and nutritional value of the fresh food as possible. High nutritional value goes hand in hand with flavor. Flavor is nature's way of telling us what is good for us. For example, fresh organic produce often tastes better than conventional commercial produce, reflecting its higher nutritional content. Also, an appealing appearance can be mean more than just good looks; the coloring of some foods is associated with the levels of nutrients in those foods. Of course, preserving basic food value (calories) is also important.

To ensure that you're retaining maximum nutritional value when drying food, keep the handling, storing and processing cycle as short as possible. It is necessary to consider the whole food handling and preparation cycle, including what is done with the food before and after it is dried. Generally, you want to keep the food handling stages to a minimum and keep the link

between harvest and consumption as direct as possible.

Cooking or blanching food is likely to have more impact on nutrient content than any other step in the food drying or handling process. If

---

Table 5-2: Fresh fruit and vegetable Handling Stages

- Harvesting
- Washing
- Temporary storage (refrigerator, countertop, or crate)
- Ripening off the vine (e.g., tomatoes, pears, plums)
- Processing (cleaning, peeling, slicing, pureeing, mixing, seasoning)
- Blanching or pre-treating
- Dehydrating in food dryer
- Storage
- Re-hydration
- Cooking or other heating
- Meal preparation
- Temporary storage
- Possible storage of leftovers (freezing, refrigeration)
- Reheating
- Disposal

you are blanching or cooking foods, do it in the shortest possible time. High temperatures associated with blanching (212° F, 100° C) destroy many nutrients, and the length of time the foods are heated has an even greater impact. Cooking is not all bad though. It increases the bioavailability (digestibility) of proteins and carbohydrates in certain foods, such as beans, and it improves the palatability of many foods.

To get the best results from your solar dryer in terms of flavor, nutrition and appearance, follow these steps:

1. Always start with the freshest, highest quality foods possible. Your dried food will only be as good as what you start with.

2. Use fruit and vegetables that are fully ripe, but not overripe. Drying will lock in the prime flavor of foods at their peak. But it is not for salvaging expired foods.

3. Skip all blanching and pre-treating of foods. Do not soak or rinse fresh foods once they have been sliced, to avoid leaching (losing) nutrients into the rinse water.

4. Put fruits and vegetables into your dryer as soon as they are processed (washed and sliced). They should be drying within ten minutes of slicing.

5. Make sure that the dryer is powered up with plenty of sunshine so that your foods will start drying right away. This may mean waiting until 9:00 or 10:00 in the morning when the sun is a little higher in the sky.

Getting off to a quick start with your drying will yield the best flavor and appearance in the end.

If you have a wet food like tomatoes or pears, you need to make significant drying progress on the first day of drying. If you get the food at least half dry the first day, it will survive the night with little problem. Once the drying process starts, it automatically begins preserving and stabilizing the food. However, if the food is started late in the day, or clouds come by, the food will still be fairly wet and the overnight stay will cause some degradation. To avoid this, use electric backup heat at night, if available.

Pre-treating Foods to Prevent Darkening

Pre-treatment of fruits to help them keep their color is usually not necessary. The darkening of fruits is not a significant problem as long as the food is fresh, not overly ripe, and is processed quickly (as described above). With a little care, it's easy to get consistently great looking and great tasting results with no additives or pre-treatment.

Some dried-food aficionados use sulfuring, sodium bisulfate, or ascorbic acid (vitamin C) to improve appearance. These pre-treatments work by preventing oxidization and stopping enzyme activity. Sulfuring and sulfating are not recommended because some people (particularly those with asthma) are allergic to sulfates. Most commercially available dried fruits are treated with sulfur compounds, so this is another advantage to drying your own. You can use an ascorbic acid dip if needed. Ascorbic acid is vitamin C and can be found in powdered or crystalline form in health and nutrition stores. Add a teaspoon of ascorbic acid to one quart of water to make a dip. Leave sliced fruit in dip for about five minutes. This process adds moisture, so you will have to increase drying time. Lemon juice is high in ascorbic acid and can be added to fruit leathers to prevent darkening.

Many food-drying books recommend blanching almost everything before drying. This is a process of partially cooking the food by steaming it or placing it briefly in boiling water. Recommended blanching times vary from one to ten minutes. The purpose is several fold:

5-7: *Solar-dried apples look and taste great without any pre-treatment*

1) to break down the cell membranes in the skin so that the food can dry faster; 2) to destroy natural enzymes that might cause food to darken; and 3) to help sterilize the food. Blanching may be necessary for commercial food-drying operations, but generally not for your own domestic use.

As an experiment, I used an electric food dryer to run a comparison test of blanched versus raw foods using green beans and cauliflower. Both vegetables were washed and sliced into 1½-inch pieces. The blanched food was steamed on high heat for about three minutes before putting it in the dryer; the other half went straight in the dryer raw. Results: There was no discernable difference in drying time between the two batches. When fully dried, the non-blanched (raw) green beans were clearly better looking, with a bright green color, while the blanched beans were darker and less appealing. The blanched cauliflower also came out darker than the raw. Flavor was comparable.

Blanching destroys nutrients, such as vitamin C. It adds more work and time to the drying process and consumes more energy. Rinsing fruits and vegetables should be sufficient, and sterilizing them with blanching is not necessary. So use blanching only if you can't get a satisfactory result with drying the raw food.

One fruit that may drive you to blanching is grapes. The skins of grapes are incredibly impervious to moisture. This is how grapes can be so juicy in the hot, dry climate where they thrive. Grapes can take up to a week to dry and may sit in your dryer for two or three days without any apparent change. Blanching will destroy the integrity of the tough grape skins and speed up the drying process. Alternatively you can cut or slightly crush the grapes to open them up.

Table 5-3: Effect of Blanching on Vitamin C	
Process	**Percent loss**
Steam blanching	16-26%
Water blanching	16-58%

Source: Effects of Food Processing on Nutritive Values, *Food Technology, December 1986.*

CHAPTER 6

Favorite Dried Food Recipes

The following pages will provide a few of my favorite dried food recipes to help you make good use of those outstanding solar-dried fruits and vegetables. If you want more recipes for your dried foods, you will find plenty in the cookbooks listed in *Resources* in Appendix E.

Solar-Dried Tomato Pesto

Here's a quick and easy recipe for a rich, tasty, tomato pesto that works as a great spread on French bread or crackers as a simple snack, or mixed into your favorite pasta. It's so good you'll want to dry all the tomatoes you can this summer. Makes about one pint.

Ingredients:

2 cups dried tomatoes, packed lightly (about 6-10 oz. depending on dryness)
1 cup walnuts, halved or chopped (about 4oz.)

¾ cup extra virgin olive oil
⅓ cup grated Parmesan cheese
5 whole garlic cloves
2 tablespoons red wine vinegar
1 tablespoon water (if tomatoes are very dry)
½ teaspoon sea salt

Add all ingredients to food processor bowl and blend until it reaches a thick, but fairly smooth, consistency. Presto, it's pesto! Stir into hot pasta noodles (spaghetti or angel hair) and add your favorite toppings.

6-1: *Tomato pesto is one way to be popular!*

Fruity Zucchini Bread

This recipe is a hearty and tasty quick bread and a great way to use last summer's bumper crop of zucchinis that you dried, along with your favorite dried fruits. You can substitute fresh fruit and zucchini for dried, if desired, but adjust moisture and cooking time accordingly. Fresh zucchini is 94 percent water, so dried zucchini is highly concentrated. You will find that two pounds of garden zucchini dries to a mere two or three ounces!

Dry ingredients

½ cup dried shredded
    zucchini, or finely chopped dried sliced
    zucchini (this is about 2 oz. of very dry
    zucchini — equivalent to about 2
    pounds of fresh zucchini, or 4 cups
    grated fresh zucchini)
2½ cups whole wheat flour
½ cup walnuts, chopped
1 cup dried fruit (mix raisins or dried
    blueberries and your favorite finely
    chopped fruit, such as peaches,
    pineapples, and apples)
1½ teaspoons baking powder
1 teaspoon baking soda
1 teaspoon cinnamon
½ teaspoon nutmeg
½ teaspoon salt

Wet ingredients

3 eggs
¾ cup canola oil
¾ cup honey
½ cup soy milk (or
    regular milk)
2 teaspoons vanilla extract

Preheat oven to 350° F. Mix all dried ingredients in a large bowl. Mix all wet ingredients in a medium bowl until blended. Add wet ingredients to dry ingredients and mix until just blended. Place in oiled loaf pan and bake for 1 hour. Let cool for 10 minutes before slicing.

6-2: *This zucchini bread is hard to photograph because it disappears so fast*

Banana Delights

(Contributed by Judi White, Hawaii)

A delicious, nutritious treat that makes a great snack or mini powerbar. "My children were raised on this great candy substitute," says Judi. "I love the sesame seed/banana flavor, but I have made this with almonds and cashews or whatever is on hand, so you can experiment with the nuts and type of nut butter used." Makes about 17 nuggets.

Ingredients:

1 cup packed dried bananas (8 oz. weighed)

3 tablespoons raw sunflower seeds

3 tablespoons raw sesame seeds

1 tablespoon peanut butter

¼ cup (approx.) dried, shredded, unsweetened coconut

Put the raw sesame seeds in the bowl of a food processor and blend until like a flour. This will take a while, and they won't break down completely. Then add the raw sunflower seeds and continue blending until the sunflower seeds are finely blended. You do not need to reduce them completely to flour. Remove this seed mixture and place in a bowl for now.

Chop the dried bananas into 1-inch pieces and measure 1 cup, firmly packed. Blend in the food processor until they form a ball. Break the ball of banana apart and blend once more until it again forms a ball. Break apart and add the chopped seeds back into the processor. Add the peanut butter and blend the mixture again until it becomes slightly crumbly.

Place the dried coconut on a plate. Take one heaping tablespoon of the banana mixture, firmly pack it into a small log shape about 1½ inch long, and firmly roll the "log" in the coconut. Don't be afraid to pack it in the coconut to provide a thick coating. Store in the refrigerator or vacuum pack and freeze for later.

6-3: *Banana delights*

Banana Sesame Chews

(Contributed by Judi White, Hawaii)

This family favorite is a thick, nutty, fruit leather that can be sliced into convenient, bite-sized squares or strips.

Ingredients:

6 ripe, raw, undried bananas
(3½ cups pureed)
¾ cup raw sesame seeds
(brown or white)

Grind raw sesame seeds into a flour-like consistency in a food processor. This may take some time, and they will not break down completely. Remove to a bowl for later. Puree the bananas in the processor until they are smooth. Add the ground sesame seeds and blend well.

Spread the mixture on a cookie sheet. Be sure to use either a stainless steel, glass or nonstick Teflon cookie sheet so that you will be able to peel it off later. You can also use Teflon-coated plastic sheets placed on any ordinary cookie sheet (see *Resources* in Appendix E for more information). Spread in a square about ¼-inch thick (about a 13-inch square). Place in the dryer and leave until the mixture sets enough to slice into 2-inch squares. This usually takes half of a sunny day in Hawaii. Do not dry completely on the cookie sheet as the mixture will stick, and it will be very hard to remove.

Use a spatula to remove the squares from the cookie sheet and place directly on the dryer screen to finish drying (putting the previously exposed side down on the screen). Dry until chewy and store in the refrigerator. Often this whole process could be completed in one day of full sun. The sesame seeds make this a calcium-rich snack for young and old.

6-4: *Banana chews*

Power Muesli

This breakfast cereal is a hearty blend of nutritious whole grains, nuts, and fruits that will get your day off to a solid start. Power Muesli provides the balance of food energy (carbohydrates, fats, proteins, and fiber) necessary for a rigorous morning of hiking or backpacking, or just to keep you going strong at the office well beyond the average commercial cereal.

The main ingredients are rolled oats and rolled rye. These grains taste great without any roasting or precooking. I love the taste of rolled rye, but if you don't like it, substitute an equal amount of the oats. Place these uncooked grains in the freezer for 48 hours to make sure there are no living organisms that could ruin your food.

I use organic grains and nuts when available. The seeds and nuts add flavor and provide the long-lasting energy, and the dried fruits from your food dryer sweeten and flavor the Muesli for an appealing taste without adding sugar.

This recipe is a great way to take advantage of your dried apples, pears, or grapes. Dried apples are one of the most expensive dried foods in the store, but are one of the easiest to make in your dryer — and they taste great in cereal. Dried pears are hard to find in stores, so you'll have to make your own. If you buy your grains and nuts in bulk, this recipe makes a complete breakfast for about 35 cents a day.

Ingredients for six pounds of Muesli:

Servings: about 25 to 30 1-cup servings

2 lbs. rolled oats

2 lbs. rolled rye

½ lb. almonds (raw) or substitute hazelnuts

⅓ lb. sunflower seeds (hulled, whole, raw)

¼ lb. wheat germ (raw)

¼ lb. sesame seeds (hulled, whole, raw)

1 lb. dried fruit (your choice or mix of apples, pears, and raisins)

For best flavor, roast almonds, sunflower seeds, sesame seeds, and wheat germ. Spread nuts and seeds on baking pans and roast them in the oven at 325° F for about 30-40 minutes, or until your nose lets you know they are done. Stir occasionally for even roasting and take care not to burn them.

Let the nuts and seeds cool off. Use a food processor or blender to chop the nuts and sunflower seeds to the desired size. Chopping makes the Muesli easier to eat and improves digestibility.

Chop fruit to desired size using hand chopper or food processor (raisins don't need chopping). Note that you may have to do this by hand because dried fruits can gum up your processor, rendering it ineffective.

Thoroughly mix all ingredients in a large bowl. Place in sealed storage containers. It's ready to eat! Just add milk (try rice milk for a little extra sweetness). If the grains or dried fruits are too hard for you, just let it soak in the milk for ten minutes before eating.

It's so good you will be excited to wake up in the morning!

Storage note: Once roasted, nuts and seeds should be eaten within about four weeks to ensure that they don't become rancid and lose flavor and nutrients. If you can't eat this much Muesli in a month, put the extra in a jar or plastic storage bag right away and freeze until needed.

Chunky Dried Vegetable Soup

This soup stock is based on your solar-dried tomatoes and can include a variety of your favorite dried veggies and herbs from the garden.

Ingredients:
1 cup dried tomatoes (3-4 oz., depending on dryness)
1 cup of your favorite dried vegetables (green beans, sweet peas, carrots, green peppers, zucchini, summer squash, corn, broccoli, cauliflower, mushrooms)
1 dried onion, chopped
4 cloves garlic
⅓ cup olive oil
1 tablespoon vinegar (or lemon juice)
½ teaspoon sea salt
Your choice of fresh or dried herbs (fennel, rosemary, oregano, lovage or celery, basil, thyme, dill, parsley, etc., to taste
4 cups water

Coarsely chop tomatoes and set aside. In a large saucepan add olive oil, finely sliced garlic cloves, and chopped dried onion. Sauté on low heat for five minutes. Add water and tomatoes and heat on high until it starts boiling. Turn down to low heat and simmer. Add all dried vegetables, salt, vinegar and half of your herbs. Continue to simmer on low for 30 minutes partially covered, or until vegetables are mostly hydrated. Turn off heat, and add remaining herbs. Let stand for another 30 minutes. Add salt and fresh ground pepper to taste.

Optional: Add cooked beans or rice to the soup for a heartier meal.

Pemmican

In many ways pemmican is the ultimate dried food product. For the bold and adventurous, try this pemmican recipe to see how Native Americans preserved food.

Pemmican was the most important food staple for the Plains Native Americans. It was a mixture of pounded dried meat, dried berries or fruit, occasionally seeds or nuts, and rendered buffalo fat, which held the mixture together and helped to seal and preserve it. Pemmican was a concentrated, high-quality food, full of protein and energy. It was both lightweight and kept for a long time without spoiling. These qualities, and the vitamin C from the fruit, made it the perfect power-food for surviving tough winters and traveling long distances in search of buffalo or game. The Plains tribes carried pemmican in parfleches, (pronounced par flesh), decorated rawhide packs strapped to their horses. Many Native American groups made pemmican, and early European explorers and fur trappers relied on it heavily.

Ingredients:

2 oz. dried buffalo meat or venison
   (substitute beef or turkey jerky)
handful of dried cherries
small handful dried blueberries or
   currants (substitute raisins or prunes)
small handful of sunflower seeds or
   nuts of any kind

2 tablespoons rendered buffalo fat
   (substitute butter or vegetable
   shortening)

Grind the dried meat jerky in a food processor or blender until finely chopped. Add the sunflower seeds and grind again. Add dried cherries and raisins (or other dried fruit) and grind finely. Place mixture in bowl. Melt the fat (or butter or shortening) and pour over mixture. Mix thoroughly with a spoon.

Empty the mixture onto a sheet of wax paper and lay another sheet of wax paper on top. With a rolling pin, flatten the pemmican into about a ⅛-inch-thick pancake.

Let the pemmican cool in the refrigerator. Voila, your own Native American-style "power-bars." Break off pieces to eat as a snack or toss into boiling water to make trail soup. Store leftover pemmican in a modern *parfleche* (sealed container or plastic bag) in a cool place.

Sun Path Charts

Sun path charts tell you where the sun will be in the sky at any time of day throughout the year. Instructions for using these charts can be found in Chapter 2 under *Geography and Seasons*. Sun paths are different for each latitude (distance from equator), so charts are provided for every 5° of latitude from 30° north to 50° north, covering most of the Lower 48 states and southern Canada. The sun's path is the same for all locations along the same latitude.

The sun's travel in the southern hemisphere is a mirror image of the northern hemisphere. The sun path chart can be used for the same latitudes in the southern hemisphere by changing the south bearing angle to north, switching east and west, and reversing the seasons.

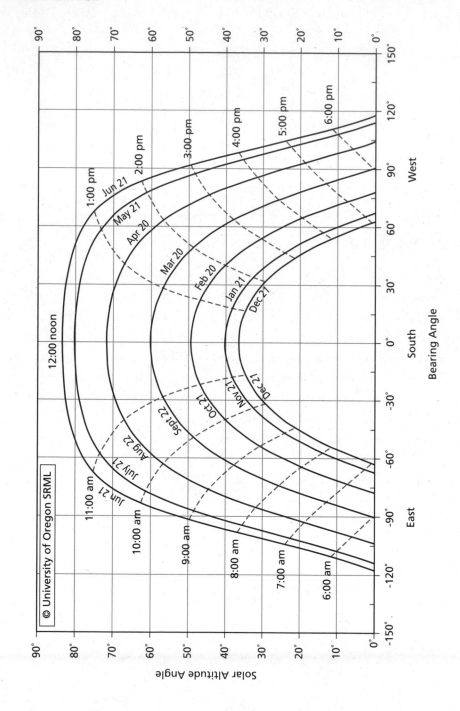

Sun Path Chart - Latitude = 30°

© University of Oregon SRML

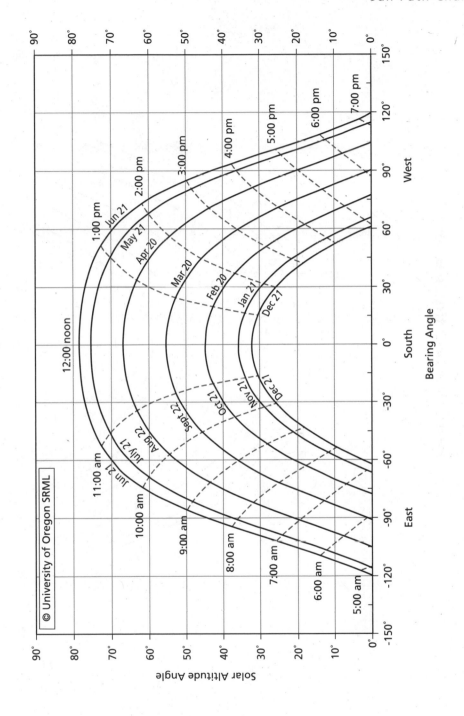

Sun Path Chart - Latitude = 35°

© University of Oregon SRML

12:00 noon

1:00 pm
Jun 21
2:00 pm
May 21
Apr 20
3:00 pm
Mar 20
4:00 pm
Feb 20
Jan 21
5:00 pm
Dec 21
6:00 pm
7:00 pm

11:00 am
Jun 21
July 21
Aug 22
10:00 am
Sept 22
9:00 am
Oct 21
Nov 21
8:00 am
Dec 21
7:00 am
6:00 am
5:00 am

Dec 21
Nov 21
Oct 21
Sept 22

Solar Altitude Angle

East
South
West

Bearing Angle

Sun Path Chart - Latitude = 40°

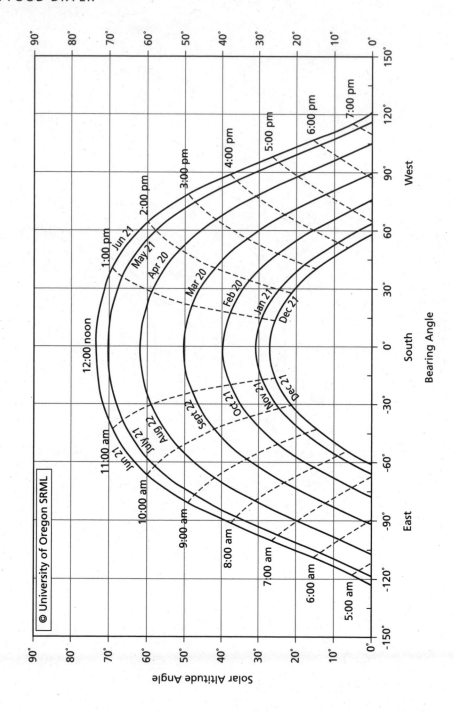

© University of Oregon SRML

Sun Path Chart - Latitude = 45°

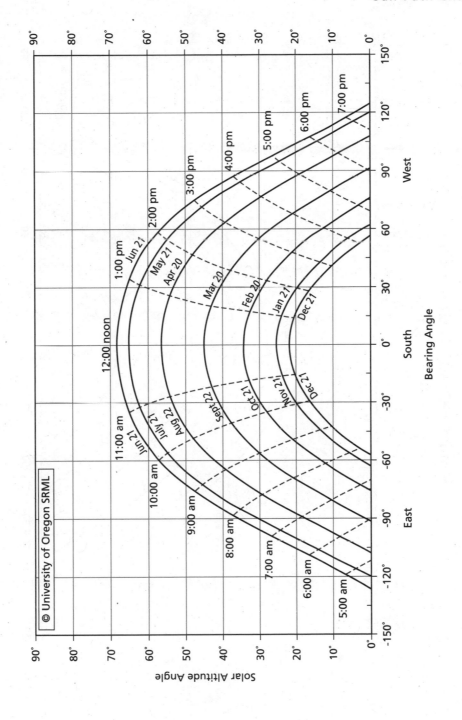

© University of Oregon SRML

Sun Path Chart - Latitude = 50°

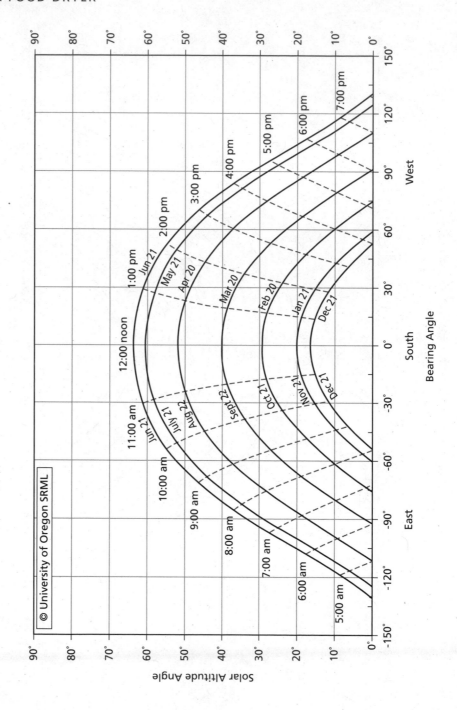

© University of Oregon SRML

Solar Altitude Angle

Bearing Angle

Useful Solar Data

The maps in this appendix provide actual daily solar energy totals from monitoring sites around the United States. The daily totals are the averages for the period shown. These average figures are useful in comparing one area with another, but keep in mind that they include overcast and rainy days, as well as sunny days. Since you will be drying food on sunny days, these figures are lower than you will experience in practice. Maps are provided for June, September to give a range suitable for the main food drying season.

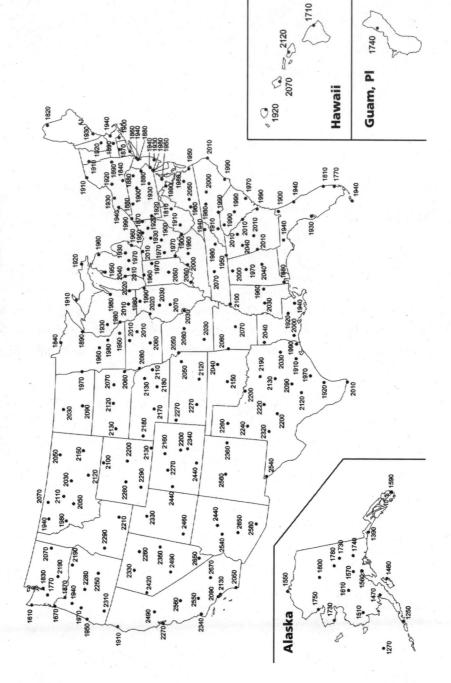

Daily Solar Radiation on a Horizontal Surface

Average for Month (Btu/ft²/day) JUNE

Source: National Renewable Energy Laboratory Resource Assessment Program

Daily Solar Radiation on a Horizontal Surface

Average for Month (Btu/ft²/day) SEPTEMBER

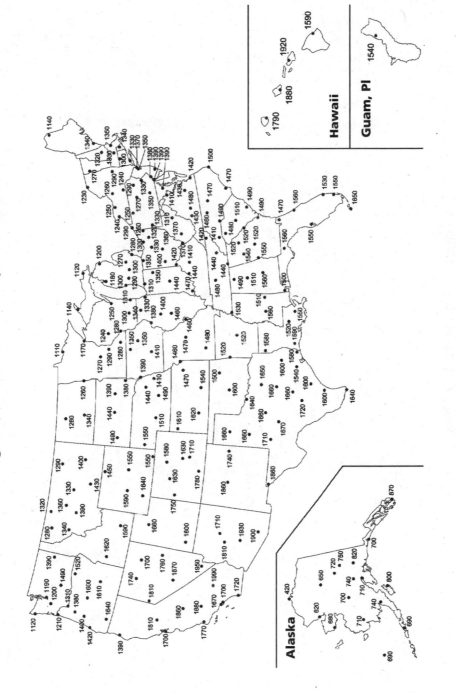

Hawaii

Guam, PI

Alaska

Source: *National Renewable Energy Laboratory Resource Assessment Program*

Daily Solar Radiation on a Horizontal Surface

Daily Average (Btu/ft²/day) **ANNUAL**

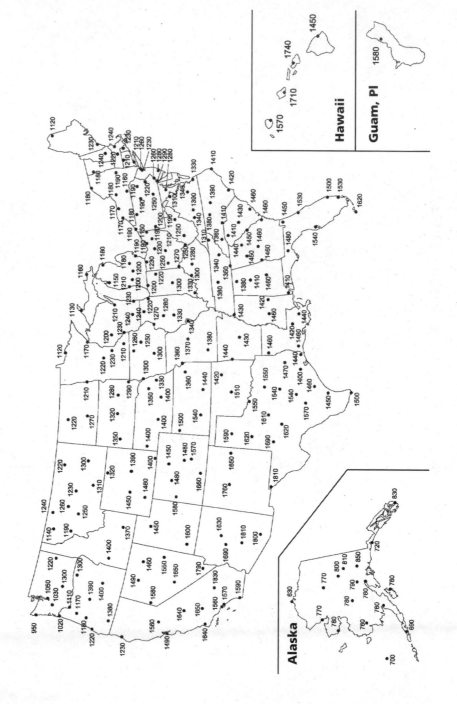

Hawaii

Guam, PI

Alaska

Source: *National Renewable Energy Laboratory Resource Assessment Program*

Handy Conversion Factors for Solar Energy

To Convert	Into	Multiply by
Energy:		
Btus	Watt-hours	0.293
Btus	kilowatt-hours	0.000293
Watt-hours	Btus	3.413
kilowatt-hours	Btus	3413
Power (radiant energy flow):		
Btus/hour per square foot	Watts per square meter	3.154
Btus/hour per square foot	kilowatts per square meter	0.00315
kilowatts per square meter	Btus/hour per square foot	317
Watts per square meter	Btus/hour per square foot	0.317
Distance:		
centimeters	inches	0.394
inches	centimeters	2.54
feet	meters	0.305
meters	feet	3.281

To Convert	Into	Multiply by
Area:		
square feet	square meters	0.0929
square meters	square feet	10.76
Weight:		
pounds (lbs)	kilograms	0.4536
kilograms	pounds (lbs)	2.205
Temperature:		
degrees Celsius (C)	Fahrenheit (F)	°C x 1.8 + 32
degrees Fahrenheit (F)	Celsius (C)	(°F - 32) x 0.5556

Glossary of Terms for Solar Energy

Altitude Angle (Solar): The angle of the sun above the horizon. Directly overhead is 90° and the horizon is 0°.

Ambient Air Temperature: Temperature of the air surrounding any object being considered.

Angle of Incidence: The angle at which a ray of light or sunshine strikes a surface. For example, a surface that directly faces the sun has a solar angle of incidence of zero. Incidence angle can go up to 90°, in which case the direction of the ray is parallel to the surface being considered.

Azimuth Angle (solar): The angle between due south and the horizontal position of the sun. If the sun is in the east or west, azimuth angle is 90°. Due south is 0° and north is 180°.

(Note: some scientists use north as 0° and south as 180°.) Similar to a compass or bearing angle.

Btu (British Thermal Unit): A unit of energy which is defined by the energy required to heat one pound of water 1° F. One Btu equals 252 calories or 0.293 watt-hours. It is said to be about the energy emitted from burning a kitchen match.

Convection: Heat transferred by the movement of a fluid (like air or water) across a surface that is at a different temperature. (See *Natural Convection*).

Diffuse Sky Radiation: The component of solar radiation received on a surface that has been scattered by dust and water vapor in the atmosphere and reflected down to Earth.

Diffuse radiation comes from the whole sky area.

Direct (or Beam) Radiation: Solar radiation received on a surface that comes directly from the sun (it passes directly through the atmosphere, and is not diffused or reflected).

Direct Gain: The transmission of solar energy through a glazing and into a space where it is converted to heat by absorption on interior surfaces.

Equinox: Either of two dates during the year when the sun's path is directly over the equator and the length of day and night are approximately equal. The vernal (spring) equinox is around March 21 and the autumnal (fall) equinox is around September 21. The equinoxes are the only days in which the sun rises due east and sets due west for every location on the earth.

Flux: The rate of flow of energy in the form of light or other radiant energy to a receiving surface.

Glazing: A generic term used for any clear or translucent sheet of material such as glass or plastic. Also refers to the glass area of a window or door.

Global Solar Radiation: Total incident solar radiation. Includes all direct, diffuse sky and diffuse reflected solar radiation received on a surface.

Insolation: See *Global Solar Radiation*.

Latitude: The angular distance north or south from the equator. The equator is 0°, the North Pole is 90° north latitude and the South Pole is 90° south latitude. Latitude lines run parallel to the equator.

Longitude: The angular distance of a location on the Earth's surface east or west of the Prime Meridian (0°). Longitude lines run north-south. The Prime Meridian runs through the Greenwich Observatory in England.

Natural Convection: The flow of a fluid (air or water) which is caused by buoyancy differences due to temperature differences within the fluid. Warmer air is lighter and less dense than cold air (i.e., hot air rises). Temperature differences are created by a hot or cold surface. No mechanical means (like a fan) is needed to move the air.

Passive Solar System: A solar-powered heating or cooling system that does not use or rely on outside mechanical or electrical inputs to operate. Passive solar systems typically heat, cool or ventilate a space. A south-facing window on a house can act as a simple passive solar heating system during the winter months. A system requiring mechanical fans, motors or pumps to operate would be an *active* solar system.

Sol-Air Temperature: The effective temperature of the surface of an object sitting outdoors in direct sunlight. This is the difference between sitting in the shade and sitting in the sun. The sunshine is typically about 20° F (11° C) warmer than the shade. Weather temperatures are always measured in the shade (for consistency).

Solar Absorptance: The fraction of incident solar radiation absorbed by a surface. The range is 0 to 1.0 (corresponding to 0 to 100 percent).

Solar Collector: Any device that captures solar energy for use, ranging from a simple window to complex photovoltaic systems.

Solar Constant: The extraterrestrial solar radiation on one square meter of area, received at the limit of the Earth's atmosphere, or 1,367 W/m². It is actually not a "constant" since it varies by ±3 percent depending on Earth's distance from the sun during its elliptical orbit and the activity of solar flares.

Solar Energy Transmittance: The percentage of solar energy from the entire solar spectrum (ultraviolet, visible and near infrared energy) that is transmitted through a glass or other glazing material. When sunlight strikes glass, solar energy is either transmitted through the pane of glass, absorbed by the glass or reflected away from the glass.

Solar Heat Gain Coefficient (SHGC): Defines the fraction of solar radiation admitted through glass both directly transmitted and absorbed and subsequently released inward. A coefficient of 1.0 represents 100 percent gain. The lower the value, the less heat is transmitted through the glass.

Solar Thermal Systems: Refers to systems that convert solar energy into heat, such as a solar hot water heater. By contrast, a solar electric system would convert solar energy into electricity as a photovoltaic system does.

Sunlight: The visible portion of the solar spectrum, excluding ultraviolet and infrared.

Solar Radiation: Radiation emitted by the sun, including the full solar spectrum.

Solar Time: The time of day adjusted so that 12 noon is when the sun is due south and highest in the sky.

Solar Spectrum: The full solar wavelength range (300-2,500 nanometers) that reaches the Earth's surface (includes ultraviolet, visible, and near infrared).

Solar Flux: The rate of flow of solar energy to a surface (see *Flux*).

Solstice: The dates of the longest and shortest days of the year. For the northern hemisphere, summer solstice is usually on or around June 21 and is the day on which the sun is highest in the sky at noon (highest altitude angle). The winter solstice is on or about December 21 and is the day with the lowest sun altitude angle. The opposite occurs in the southern hemisphere.

Tropic of Cancer: A latitude line of 23.5° north of the equator, which is the northernmost point where the sun reaches directly overhead (during summer solstice).

Tropic of Capricorn: A latitude line of 23.5° south of the equator, which is the southern-most point where the sun reaches directly overhead (during winter solstice).

Ultraviolet Radiation (UV): electromagnetic radiation with wavelengths shorter than visible light (less than 380 nanometers) and longer than x-rays.

Visible Spectrum (light): The wavelengths of radiation that are visible to the human eye (380 to 780 nanometers).

Zenith: highest point of the sky hemisphere, i.e., the point vertically above the observer (an altitude angle of 90°).

Zenith Angle: The angle between the direction of interest (of the sun, for example) and the zenith (directly overhead).

Resources for Solar Food Drying

For additional resources, design updates and more ideas for using and enhancing your solar dryer, visit <www.solarfooddryer.com>.

Food Drying Books with Dried Food Recipes

Complete Dehydrator Cookbook, by Mary Bell and Evie Righter, William Morrow & Company, Inc., NY, 1994, hardcover, 304 pages. A good, comprehensive book on food drying with lots of good recipes and tips for using dried foods. Many good recipes for backpackers. Not illustrated. Focus on electric drying, but mentions other methods.

Dry It: You'll Like It! by Gen MacManiman, published by MacManiman, Inc., Living Foods Dehydrators, 3023 362nd Ave. S.E., Fall City, Washington 98024, 2000, 75 pages, $10, phone 425-222-5587 or <www.dryit.com>.

Includes recipes and general drying guidelines for low-temperature "raw food" drying. Book includes plans for building an electric food dryer. There is no information on using solar; however, plans are available for a solar heating design that can be added to the electric dryer (ask for catalog).

How to Dry Foods, by Deanna DeLong, HPBooks, New York, NY, 2nd edition, 1992, 160 pages. Good overview of food drying with photos and recipes. Focus on electric drying but briefly mentions solar drying.

Trail Food: Drying and Cooking Food for Backpacking and Paddling, by Alan S. Kesselheim, International Marine/Mountain Press, 1998, 112 pages. Good ideas for eating well in the outdoors using lightweight dried foods.

Food Drying Accessories

Thermometers (bi-metal stem-type with dial):

Miller Thermometer Company, Inc.
Hartford, Michigan 1-800-922-3124
www.millerthermometer.com/
BimetalDialsize.htm

Old-Fashioned Apple Peeler-Slicer-Corer

This handy one-step apple processor is now available at many stores including those listed below. Some are equipped with a clamp base and some with a suction base; depending on where you will be using it, you can choose the best securing system. With the clamp base, you can attach the peeler-slicer-corer to a cutting board over the sink for easy cleanup.

- Excalibur Dehydrator (clamp base): www.excaliburdehydrator.com/cat7.htm
- Mending Shed (clamp base): http://shop.store.yahoo.com/ mendingshed/applepeeler2.html
- The Vermont Country Store: www.vermontcountrystore.com/
- Chef's Resource: www.chefsresource.com/vl340.html
- Target: www.target.com

Food-Safe Polypropylene Screens and Non-Stick Teflon Sheets for Fruit Roll-Ups

Living Foods Dehydrators
www.dryit.com

3023 362nd Ave. S.E.
Fall City, WA 98024
1-800-609-2160 or 425-222-0896

Excalibur Products (A Division of KBI)
www.excaliburdehydrator.com/
6083 Power Inn Road
Sacramento, CA 95824
1-800-875-4254
or 916-381-4254

See www.solarfooddryer.com for more food screen sources.

Solar Drying Articles

- "The Design, Construction, and Use of an Indirect, Through-Pass, Solar Food Dryer," Dennis Scanlin, *Home Power Magazine*, Issue #57, February / March 1997
- "Improving Solar Food Dryers," Dennis Scanlin, Marcus Renner, David Domermuth, & Heath Moody, *Home Power Magazine*, Issue #69, February / March 1999

Home Power Magazine
http://www.homepower.com
PO Box 520, Ashland, OR 97520
1-800-707-6585
541-512-0343 (Outside USA)
hp@homepower.com

Solar Energy Resources

Sun Path Charts
University of Oregon Solar Radiation
Monitoring Laboratory:

http://solardat.uoregon.edu/
SunChartProgram.html
This website will create a custom sun path chart showing the location of the sun in the sky for any time of year for the latitude of your location. Input your latitude (find this on a local road map or atlas) and use "solar time." Solar time is noon when the sun is at its highest point in the sky.

American Solar Energy Society
www.ases.org
2400 Central Ave., Suite A,
Boulder, CO 80301
303-443-3130
ases@ases.org

Solar Today Magazine:
www.solartoday.org

Solar Accessories

Sun-Lite HP fiberglass glazing
Solar Components Corporation
(Kalwall Corp.)

www.solar-components.com
121 Valley Street,
Manchester, NH 03103-6211
603-668-8186
solar2@ix.netcom.com

Internet Resources

National Center for Home Food Preservation has links to state cooperative extensions and some food drying literature (mostly related to canning):
www.uga.edu/nchfp/index.html

Living Foods Dehydrators has a good website with recipes, advice and some accessories:
www.dryit.com/

The Solar Cooking Archive has more ways to enjoy the sun: solarcooking.org/

Index

A

absorber plate, 24-25, 40, 42-43, 49, 51
    assembly, 52-53, 68
air flow, 21-22, 26, 28, 35-38, 39, 43, 44
altitude angle, 10, 11, 13, 98, 100, 102, 109
aluminum tape, 52, 68, 69, 74
Appalachian food dryer, 37-39
Aprovecho Research Center, 44-45
assembly. *See* SunWorks SFD

B

backup electric heat, 6, 17, 30, 39, 44, 47, 87
    assembly, 52, 64-65, 68-69
    SunWorks SFD, 44, 52, 80
building materials, 31-34. *See also* SunWorks
    SFD

C

climate and weather, 6, 15, 17, 22, 37, 39, 111
    changes, 31, 34, 79-80

D

Delta-T, 21-22, 80
direct heating, 22-24, 40-41, 43, 48
double glazing, 29, 49
dried food
    favorites, 77
    storing, 24, 83.
    See also recipes
dryer cabinet, 30, 36-39, 42, 50
    assembly, 49, 54-74
    materials, 34, 41, 50-52
drying temperatures, 21-23, 26, 29, 33, 80-82,
    115
drying time, 79-80

E

Earth, the
    atmosphere of, 17-19, 109, 110, 111
    hemispheres of, 11, 14-15, 26, 19, 97, 112
    rotation of, 14-15

tilt of, 14-15
electric food dryers, 3-4, 7

F
fiberglass
 reinforced polyester, 32
 screens, 33, 50, 51
 glazing, 40
food
 pre-treating, 85-86, 87-89
 preparation, 77-79
 preservation, 81-82, 83
 temperature, 82-83. *See also* recipes
food safety, 21, 30, 33, 50-51
food screens, 33-34, 41, 44, 50-51, 74, 79, 114
fruit. *See* food; nutrition; recipes

G
glazing, 25, 29, 39, 40, 49, 110
 assembly, 73-74
 cleaning, 31, 80-81
 materials, 32-33, 48, 50, 51, 115
 recycled, 34, 49

H
hardware, 51, 72
hot box, 34-37
humidity, 6, 22, 35, 80

I
indirect heat, 23-24, 39, 43
insulation, 29

L
latitudes, 10-12, 14, 97, 110, 115.
 See also sun path charts

M
Maui fruit dryer, 35
metric conversions, 18, 107-108
Mylar, 33

N
Native Americans, 4, 5, 34, 95
natural convection, 5, 26, 110
New Mexico dryer, 40-41
nutrition, 24, 78, 84-86, 88

O
open-air sun drying.
 See sun drying
operating tips, 80-81
outdoor temperature, 6, 17, 21-23, 79-82,
 113

P
pest prevention, 29-31
plastic films, 32-33
Plexiglass, 32
polycarbonate sheet, 32
polyethylene, 33
polypropylene screens, 33, 34, 50-51
plywood, 29, 31, 49, 51
 cutting, 54-59

R

radiation, 15-17, 18-19, 28
    averages, 104-106
    square, 16-17
recipes, 89-96, 113
    banana delights, 92
    banana sesame chews, 93
    chunky dried vegetable soup, 95
    fruity zucchini bread, 91
    pemmican, 95-96
    power muesli, 94-95
    solar-dried tomato pesto, 90
recycled materials, 6, 34, 49
reflectors, 29
resources, 113-115
Rodale Plans, 39-40

S

sol-air temperature, 22, 82, 111
solar altitude angles, 10, 11, 13, 19. *See also* sun
    path charts
solar collector, 24-27, 38, 111
solar energy, 9-19
    charts and data, 103-108
    daily chart, 28
    and geography, 10-12, 27
    and latitude, 10-11
    seasonality, 11-12, 14, 17, 26-29, 79
solar fan, 5, 26, 43
solar food dryer
    advantages, 3, 7
    design elements, 21-45

history of, 6-7
    maintenance, 30-31, 80-81
    materials, 31-34
    tilt angle, 25-29. *See also* SunWorks SFD
solar photovoltaic systems, 27, 125
solar time, 14, 111
solar water heating, 24-25, 27, 29
solar weed killer, 9
stainless steel screens, 33
sun angles. *See* solar altitude angles
sun drying, 5, 22-23, 34
sun path charts, 12-14, 97-102
SunWorks SFD
    assembly, 52-75
    capacity, 31, 79
    design, 7, 41-45
    features, 47-50
    materials, 29, 47, 50-51

T

temperature. *See* drying temperatures; sol-air
    temperature
thermometer, 52, 66, 74, 82, 114
tools, 47, 50

V

vents, 22, 26, 35-38, 43-44, 47, 51, 80, 81
assembly, 67-71
vegetables. *See* food; recipes

W

weatherproofing, 29, 51, 73

About the Author

Eben Fodor

I've been a sun worshiper since I was a kid, spending every possible minute outdoors (though now mostly covered up with sunscreen or a hat). Energy conservation, energy efficiency and renewable energies were my first professional passion. I studied mechanical engineering at the University of Wisconsin so I could re-invent the steam-powered automobile to run on renewable energy. Just throw a few chunks of wood in the furnace (located in the trunk) and off you go! This led to a 15-year career in the energy field working on residential and commercial energy conservation and alternative energies such as ethanol, solar, wind and biomass. I worked on high-efficiency heating systems and designed and built several passive solar systems.

I completed graduate work at the University of Oregon in environmental studies and urban planning, where I became interested in land use, particularly our preoccupation with paving it. I started working in the land use and growth management field, mostly for non-profits and community groups trying to stop or scale back harmful developments. This experience led to my first book, *Better Not Bigger: How to Take Control of Urban Growth and Improve Your Community*, which has become the unofficial slow-growth handbook of land-use activism.

Related research, writing, speaking, and consulting work have kept me busy since.

I love organic gardening of both vegetables and fruits, as well as landscaping with native plants. My wife and I eat mostly organic produce that we either grow or buy from local farmers. Food dehydrating was an obvious way to preserve more of the high-quality, locally-grown foods we thrive on.

Websites: www.solarfooddryer.com and www.FodorandAssociates.com

Also by Eben Fodor

Better Not Bigger

How to Take Control of Urban Growth and Improve Your Community

Eben Fodor

Better NOT Bigger, provides insights, ideas, and tools to empower citizens to switch off their local "growth machine" by debunking the pro-growth rhetoric. Highly accessible to ordinary citizens as well as professional planners.

"A manual for taking apart the machinery of hidden policies and political coalitions that drive unfettered growth in our towns and cities. Buy this book. Take it home. Read it. Then pass it on."

— Alan Durning

184 pages 5.5" x 8.5"
ISBN 0-86571-386-3
Pb US$15.95 / Can$19.95

Other books available from New Society Publishers

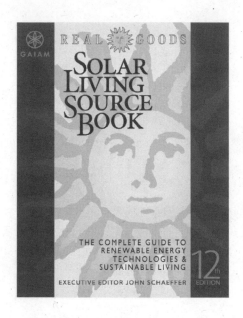

Real Goods Solar Living Sourcebook - 12th Edition

The Complete Guide to Renewable Energy Technologies & Sustainable Living

Edited by John Schaeffer

This fully updated classic of sustainable living technology gives you access to the world's most extensive selection of hardware for renewable energy, sustainable living, alternative construction, green building, homesteading, off-the-grid living and alternative transportation. This 12th edition includes several brand new and many completely rewritten sections - all the information you need to make sustainable living a reality.

544 pages 8.5 x 11"
Pb ISBN 0-91657-105-X
US$35.00 / Can $45.00

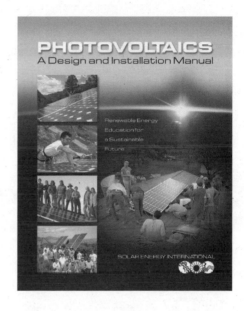

Photovoltaics

A Design and Installation Manual

Solar Energy International

Photovoltaics provides the critical information to successfully design, install and maintain PV systems. It includes an overview of photovoltaic electricity and a detailed description of PV system components; chapters on sizing photovoltaic systems, analyzing sites and installing PV systems; and details on PV system maintenance, troubleshooting and solar insolation data for over 300 sites around the world.

320 pages 8.5 x 11"
Pb ISBN 0-86571-520-3
US$59.95 / Can$74.95

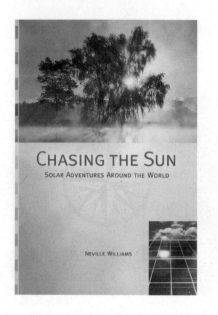

Chasing the Sun

Solar Adventures Around the World

Neville Williams

This is the fascinating account of the author's twelve year quest to bring solar power and light to people in the developing world who have no electricity. The story of the non-profit Solar Electric Light Fund (SELF) which promoted solar power for a decade by setting up pilot solar rural electrification programs in eleven developing countries, and the commercial Solar Electric Light Company that brought solar electricity to 50,000 families in India, Sri Lanka and Vietnam, this green-energy development narrative is fun and illuminating.

Neville Williams was an award-winning journalist for many years who also worked as the national media director for Greenpeace.

320 pages 6 x 9"
Pb ISBN 0-86571-537-8
US$18.95 / Can$22.95

Microhydro

Clean Power from Water

Scott Davis

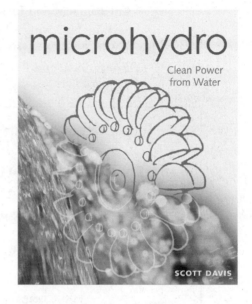

Hydroelectricity is the world's largest — and cleanest — source of renewable energy. But despite lively interest in renewables generally, there is an information vacuum about the smallest version of the technology dubbed "the simplest, most reliable and least expensive way to generate power off-grid." Highly illustrated and practical, *Microhydro* is the first complete book on the topic in a decade. Including both AC and DC systems, it covers principles, design and site considerations, equipment options, and legal, environmental, and economic factors.

176 pages / 7.5 x 9"
Mother Earth News Wiser Living Series
Pb ISBN 0-86571-484-3
US$22.95 / Can$29.95

If you have enjoyed *The Solar Food Dryer* you might also enjoy other

BOOKS TO BUILD A NEW SOCIETY

Our books provide positive solutions for people who want to
make a difference. We specialize in:

**Environment and Justice • Conscientious Commerce
Sustainable Living • Ecological Design and Planning
Natural Building & Appropriate Technology • New Forestry
Educational and Parenting Resources • Nonviolence
Progressive Leadership • Resistance and Community**

New Society Publishers

ENVIRONMENTAL BENEFITS STATEMENT

New Society Publishers has chosen to produce this book on Enviro 100, recycled paper made with **100% post consumer waste**, processed chlorine free, and old growth free.

For every 5,000 books printed, New Society saves the following resources:[1]

19	Trees
1,739	Pounds of Solid Waste
1,914	Gallons of Water
2,496	Kilowatt Hours of Electricity
3,162	Pounds of Greenhouse Gases
14	Pounds of HAPs, VOCs, and AOX Combined
5	Cubic Yards of Landfill Space

[1]Environmental benefits are calculated based on research done by the Environmental Defense Fund and other members of the Paper Task Force who study the environmental impacts of the paper industry.

For more information on this environmental benefits statement, or to inquire about environmentally friendly papers, please contact New Leaf Paper – info@newleafpaper.com Tel: 888 • 989 • 5323.

For a full list of NSP's titles, please call **1-800-567-6772** *or check out our website at:*

www.newsociety.com

NEW SOCIETY PUBLISHERS